"The theological essays in this brilliantly provocative book are timely, philosophically rich and go to the depth of the social and political controversies enlivened by COVID-19. This book is essential reading for anyone wondering what relevance theology has for current socio-ecological issues."

— *Celia Deane-Drummond, Director, Laudato Si' Research Institute, Campion Hall, University of Oxford*

"This sparkling collection of essays reveals how the turn of theology to traditional concerns with the metaphysical and the cosmic is enabling it to undertake a visionary engagement with the new extreme human and natural crisis of our time."

— *Catherine Pickstock, Norris-Hulse Professor of Divinity, University of Cambridge*

"This volume is not only timely, it is essential reading for those who want to understand how theology and theologians are responding to our all-encompassing pandemic. Provocative and suggestive for reimagining human-Earth relations."

— *Mary Evelyn Tucker, Yale Forum on Religion and Ecology*

"To say that this book is timely in a difficult and painful time is to say that it intervenes, maybe even rescues theology from failing to connect the dots between the pandemic, our ecological crisis, and the realities of oppression that also plague us. The rightly celebrated contributors to this book provide insights that help us see what must be thought and what must be done in order to keep us from the endless repetition of this suffering. Yet they also remind us what theology must look like in order not to contribute to that same suffering."

— *Willie James Jennings, Associate Professor of Systematic Theology and Africana Studies, Yale Divinity School*

"Alexander Hampton's volume is remarkable for the range and authority of its authors, and the profound way in which they address a pandemic that has upended lives and communities across the globe, and laid bare our precarious relationship to the rest of nature."

— *Andrew Davison, Starbridge Lecturer in Theology and Natural Sciences, University of Cambridge*

"As these provocative essays from some of the most creative thinkers in theology and ecology probe the meaning of the pandemic, they stimulate far-reaching conversations about inherited notions of nature, God, and humanity."

—*Willis Jenkins, Professor and Chair of Religious Studies, University of Virginia*

Pandemic, Ecology and Theology

As the sequential stages of the 2020 COVID-19 pandemic have unfolded, so have its complexities. What initially presented as a health emergency has revealed itself to be a phenomenon of many facets. It has demonstrated human creativity, the oft-neglected presence of nature, and the resilience of communities. Equally, it has exposed deep social inequities, conceptual inadequacies, and structural deficiencies about the way we organise our civilisation and our knowledge.

As the situation continues to advance, the question is whether the crisis will be grasped as an opportunity to address the deep structural, ecological, and social challenges that we brought with us into the second decade of the new millennium. This volume addresses the collective sense that the pandemic is more than a problem to manage our way out of. Rather, it is a moment to consider our broken relationship with the natural world, and our alienation from a deeper sense of purpose and meaning.

The contributors, though differing in their diagnoses and recommendations, share the belief that this moment, with its transformative possibility, not be forfeit. Equally, they share the conviction that the chief ground of any such reorientation ineluctably involves our collective engagement with both ecology and theology.

Alexander J. B. Hampton is Assistant Professor at the Department for the Study of Religion, University of Toronto, Canada.

Routledge Focus on Religion

The Bible, Social Media and Digital Culture
Peter M. Phillips

Religious Studies and the Goal of Interdisciplinarity
Brent Smith

Visual Thought in Russian Religious Philosophy
Pavel Florensky's Theory of the Icon
Clemena Antonova

American Babylon
Christianity and Democracy Before and After Trump
Philip S. Gorski

Avantgarde Art and Radical Material Theology
A Manifesto
Petra Carlsson Redell

Pandemic, Ecology and Theology
Perspectives on COVID-19
Edited by Alexander J. B. Hampton

Trump and History
Protestant Reactions to 'Make America Great Again'
Matthew Rowley

For more information about this series, please visit: https://www.routledge.com/Routledge-Focus-on-Religion/book-series/RFR

Pandemic, Ecology and Theology
Perspectives on COVID-19

Edited by
Alexander J. B. Hampton

LONDON AND NEW YORK

First published 2021
by Routledge
2 Park Square, Milton Park, Abingdon, Oxon OX14 4RN

and by Routledge
52 Vanderbilt Avenue, New York, NY 10017

Routledge is an imprint of the Taylor & Francis Group, an informa business

© 2021 selection and editorial matter, Alexander J. B. Hampton; individual chapters, the contributors

The right of Alexander J. B. Hampton to be identified as the author of the editorial material, and of the authors for their individual chapters, has been asserted in accordance with sections 77 and 78 of the Copyright, Designs and Patents Act 1988.

All rights reserved. No part of this book may be reprinted or reproduced or utilised in any form or by any electronic, mechanical, or other means, now known or hereafter invented, including photocopying and recording, or in any information storage or retrieval system, without permission in writing from the publishers.

Trademark notice: Product or corporate names may be trademarks or registered trademarks, and are used only for identification and explanation without intent to infringe.

British Library Cataloguing-in-Publication Data
A catalogue record for this book is available from the British Library

Library of Congress Cataloging-in-Publication Data
Names: Hampton, Alexander J. B., editor.
Title: Pandemic, ecology and theology : perspectives on COVID-19 / edited by Alexander J.B. Hampton.
Description: Abingdon, Oxon ; New York, NY : Routledge, 2021. | Series: Routledge focus on religion | Includes bibliographical references and index. |
Identifiers: LCCN 2020031971 (print) | LCCN 2020031972 (ebook) | ISBN 9780367615826 (hardback) | ISBN 9780367615840 (paperback) | ISBN 9781003105602 (ebook)
Subjects: LCSH: Diseases—Religious aspects—Christianity. | COVID-19 (Disease)—Religious aspects—Christianity. | Diseases—Religious aspects. | Religion—Philosophy. | Human ecology—Religious aspects—Christianity. | Human ecology—Religious aspects.
Classification: LCC BT162.D57 P37 2021 (print) | LCC BT162.D57 (ebook) | DDC 261.8/321962414—dc23
LC record available at https://lccn.loc.gov/2020031971
LC ebook record available at https://lccn.loc.gov/2020031972

ISBN: 978-0-367-61582-6 (hbk)
ISBN: 978-1-003-10560-2 (ebk)

Typeset in Times New Roman
by codeMantra

Contents

List of contributors   ix

Introduction: theology and ecology in a time of pandemic   1
ALEXANDER J. B. HAMPTON AND ANNALEA ROSE THIESSEN

1 **Viral visions and dark dreams: ecological darkness and enmeshment in the time of COVID-19**   4
JOSHUA L. I. GENTZKE

2 **Ecology and the unbuffered self: identity, agency, and authority in a time of pandemic**   17
ALEXANDER J. B. HAMPTON

3 **What happened to touch?**   29
RICHARD KEARNEY

4 **The gallop of the pale green horse: pandemic, pandemonium and panentheism**   41
CATHERINE KELLER

5 **Eschatology in a time of crisis**   54
SEAN J. McGRATH

6 **The multidimensional unity of life, theology, ecology, and COVID-19**   66
DEREK A. MICHAUD

7 Between catastrophes: God, nature and humanity 78
JOHN MILBANK

8 COVID-19, human ecology and the ontological turn to Gaia 90
MICHAEL NORTHCOTT

9 The recovery of nature's religious role in the context of the pandemic 103
WILLEMIEN OTTEN

10 Listening to the pandemic: decentering humans through silence and sound 116
LISA H. SIDERIS

Index 129

Contributors

Joshua L. I. Gentzke (Michigan State University) is Assistant Professor in the Department of Religious Studies. He specialises in mysticism, alternative spiritualties, and ecology. He is currently completing a book on Jacob Böhme, and a multimedia study of the mythopoetic and political uses of darkness in Western religious thoughts and practice.

Alexander J. B. Hampton (University of Toronto) is Assistant Professor in the Department of Religion, specialising in metaphysics, poetics, and ecology. His books include *Romanticism and the Re-Invention of Modern Religion* (Cambridge, 2019), *Christian Platonism: A History* (Cambridge, 2020), and a forthcoming study on post-secular nature. For more details on the author, please visit www.ajbhampton.com.

Richard Kearney (Boston College) holds the Charles Seelig Chair in Philosophy and has written several books on the philosophy of religion, imagination, and carnal hermeneutics. His most recent works include *Touch: Recovering our Most Vital Sense* (Columbia, 2020) and *Imagination Now: A Richard Kearney Reader* (Rowman and Littlefield, 2020).

Catherine Keller (Drew University) is George T. Cobb Professor of Constructive Theology in the Graduate Division of Religion. Her books include *Apocalypse Now and Then*, *On the Mystery*, *Cloud of the Impossible* and *Political Theology of the Earth*. Her new book, *Apocalypse After All? Climate, Democracy and Other Last Chances*, is forthcoming.

Sean J. McGrath (Memorial University) is a Professor of Philosophy and Theology. His books include *The Turn to the Positive: The Philosophical Foundations of the Late Schelling* (Edinburgh), *Thinking Nature: An Essay in Negative Ecology* (Edinburgh), and *The Dark Ground of Spirit: Schelling and the Unconscious* (Routledge).

x *Contributors*

Derek A. Michaud (University of Maine) is Lecturer in Philosophy and Coordinator of the Religious and Judaic Studies programmes. He has published on the Plotinus, Origen, Bonaventure, Nicholas of Cusa, and early modern Christian Platonism. He is the author of *Reason Turned into Sense: John Smith on Spiritual Sensation* (Peeters, 2017).

John Milbank (University of Nottingham) is Emeritus Professor of Religion, Politics, and Ethics. He previously taught at the Universities of Lancaster, Cambridge, and Virginia. He is the author of many books, including *Theology and Social Theory*, *Beyond Secular Order*, and *The Politics of Virtue* (with Adrian Pabst).

Michael Northcott (Universitas Gadjah Mada) is Visiting Professor at the Indonesian Consortium of Religious Studies, and Emeritus Professor at the University of Edinburgh. His recent publications include *A Political Theology of Climate Change* (Eerdmans, 2013) and *Place, Ecology and the Sacred* (Bloomsbury, 2015), and his forthcoming publication is *God and Gaia* (Routledge).

Willemien Otten (University of Chicago) is Professor of the History of Christianity and Theology in the Divinity School, and the director of the Martin Marty Center for the Public Understanding of Religion. Her most recent publication is *Thinking Nature and the Nature of Thinking: From Eriugena to Emerson* (Stanford, 2020).

Lisa H. Sideris (Indiana University) is Professor of Religious Studies and Associate Director of the Center for Religion and the Human. She is the author of *Environmental Ethics, Ecological Theology, and Natural Selection* (Columbia, 2003) and co-editor of *Rachel Carson: Legacy and Challenge* (SUNY, 2003) and *Consecrating Science* (University of California, 2017).

Annalea Rose Thiessen (University of Chicago) is a doctoral student at the Divinity School, with a Master of Arts in Religion and Ecology from Yale Divinity School and a BA (Honours) in History of Religions from the University of Toronto. Her research is centred on late antique theologies of creation.

Introduction
Theology and ecology in a time of pandemic

Alexander J. B. Hampton and
Annalea Rose Thiessen

As the sequential stages of the 2020 COVID-19 pandemic have unfolded, so have its complexities. What initially presented as a health emergency has revealed itself to be a phenomenon of many facets. It has demonstrated human creativity, the oft neglected presence of nature, and the resilience of communities. Equally, it has exposed deep social inequities, conceptual inadequacies, and structural deficiencies about the way we organise our civilisation and our knowledge. As the situation continues to advance, the question for many is whether the crisis will be grasped as an opportunity to address the deep structural, ecological, and social challenges that we brought with us into the second decade of the new millennium, or will we collectively, if hesitantly and reluctantly, return to the same problematic perceptions and practices that we previously held. The strange stillness of the pandemic has provided a moment for pan-reflection, and an opportunity to re-orientate the status quo. For many, there is a collective sense that this is more than an issue to manage our way out of. Rather, it is indicative of our broken relationship with the natural world of which we should be a part, and perhaps our alienation from a deeper sense of meaning, one not centred exclusively upon human needs and wants.

The contributors to this volume, though differing in their diagnoses and recommendations, share the belief that this moment, with its transformative possibility, not be forfeit. Equally, they share the conviction that the chief ground of any such reorientation ineluctably involves our collective engagement with both ecology and theology. These two words, signifying respectively discourse (-*logia*) about home (*oikos*) and divinity (*theos*), indicate the contention that an engagement with the larger constitutive framework of meaning making, our collective social imaginary, is essential if the present sense of unease with the world as we have made it is to be turned into an opportunity for positive change. As we move into the next stage of the pandemic, the question is how to cultivate our desire for transformation into a constructive ground for re-invention, and how to do so without having these efforts collapse into the shallow ideological polarisations that too often characterise the present age.

The question of why these two frameworks, theology and ecology, and not others, might arise. In the case of the former, this can be addressed by turning to the contentious claims of Lynn White.[1] Whilst White claimed that religion, and particularly Christianity, bore much blame for the modern destructive anthropocentric conceptualisation of nature, this was not all that he argued. Perhaps just as controversially, he claimed that it was not by escaping religion that ecological crisis could be overcome. Rather, he asserted the necessity of religion in re-framing our relationship to nature. We must, he wrote, either 'find a new religion or re-think our old one'.[2] For White, religion and its secular inheritance, in both good and ill, constituted the intellectual framework that formed human attitudes and actions towards the earth. Similarly, religion is relevant to the pandemic, an ecological phenomenon, precisely because the human response to the virus, scientific and technological, social and intellectual, occurs within a conceptual framework constituted by religion and its present-day intellectual inheritance.[3]

In justifying the framework of ecology, the emergent interdisciplinary field of the environmental humanities offers some guidance. This field points out that we are already possessed of the scientific and technical knowledge to correct our broken relationship with nature, and address the century-old environmental crisis.[4] This points to the fact that what is important for realising the transformative possibility of the moment is not scientific, technological or technocratic innovation, but the context in which these solutions to the environmental crisis will be implemented. Accordingly, the environmental humanities calls for an exhaustive re-consideration of the human context or conceptual framework wherein we conceive of nature and the place of humans within it. To consider the coronavirus pandemic with reflections on ecology and theology is to recognise that all environmental science and technology takes place within a particular social imaginary that profoundly impacts human attitudes and actions upon this earth. The pandemic causes us to collectively reflect upon our inherited social imaginary with new eyes, and begin to envision alternative possibilities for the flourishing of both human and non-human life.

The varying voices of this volume, scholars in religious studies, philosophy, religion and science and theology, offer a range of perspectives that are intended to be part of a larger conversation that we hope will occur within and without the academy, and across disciplines and traditions, as we collectively engage the challenge of the pandemic. Consequently, the aim of this book is to offer an intellectually local response to a global crisis—a contribution to a much broader conversation that we hope to have as a global community. As is clear in the varied yet interconnected chapters of this volume, addressing this ongoing moment, both theologically and ecologically, allows us to consider what the pandemic crisis might reveal about a larger sense of ecological and social crisis, and how the pandemic offers an opportunity to collectively re-think our conceptual framework radically anew.

Alexander J.B. Hampton
Blackie, Alberta, Canada

Annalea Rose Thiessen
Nelson, British Columbia, Canada

Notes

1 Lynn White Jr., "The Historical Roots of Our Ecologic Crisis," *Science* 155, no. 3767 (1967), 1203–1207; Elspeth Whitney, "Lynn White Jr.'s 'the Historical Roots of Our Ecologic Crisis' after 50 Years," *History Compass* 13, no. 8 (2015), 396–410; Elspeth Whitney, "The Lynn White Thesis: Reception and Legacy," *Environmental Ethics* 35, no. 3 (2013), 313–331.
2 White, 1206.
3 See Peter Harrison, *The Bible, Protestantism, and the Rise of Natural Science* (Cambridge: Cambridge University Press, 1998); Amos Funkenstein, *Theology and the Scientific Imagination from the Middle Ages to the Seventeenth Century* (Princeton, NJ: Princeton University Press, 1986).
4 Robert S. Emmett and David E. Nye, *The Environmental Humanities: A Critical Introduction* (Cambridge, MA: The MIT Press, 2017), 7–11, 71–92; Val Plumwood, *Environmental Culture: The Ecological Crisis of Reason* (London: Routledge, 2002), 38–61; Jeremy David Bendik-Keymer and Chris Haufe, "Anthropogenic Mass Extinction: The Science, the Ethics, and the Civics," in *The Oxford Handbook of Environmental Ethics*, eds. Stephen M. Gardiner and Allen Thompson (Oxford: Oxford University Press, 2016), 427–437.

1 Viral visions and dark dreams
Ecological darkness and enmeshment in the time of COVID-19

Joshua L. I. Gentzke

COVID-19 has ushered in tenebrous times. The pandemic is truly a global event, affecting "all" (*pan*) "people" (*dêmos*). Yet the collectivity this implies—a sentiment distilled into slogans such as "we are all in this together"—obscures glaring disparities in how this situation affects communities along economic, racial, and geographic lines with a naïve holism. Nevertheless, on microscopic and macroscopic scales, the pandemic has foregrounded the precariously interconnected nature of our existence in radical ways. It has forcefully existentialized ecology by returning the questions it asks *about* reality *to* reality. But while the crisis disabuses us of the illusion of a segmented reality, wherein self, other, human, and nonhuman occupy autonomous existences, its virulence impels us to fear the very linkages it reveals.

Viewed through the lens of "ecognostics" like Timothy Morton, this radical enmeshment catalyzes an ecstatic vision wherein, "[l]ife-forms constitute a mesh that is infinite and beyond concept—unthinkable as such…too 'large' but also…infinitesimally small."[1] However from a Schopenhauerian angle, one could also characterize the shift in terms of what Eugene Thacker refers to as a "'de-scaling' of the human": a disintegration of the humanist subject into a meaningless "network of forces that course through the human in ways that function at once at the macro-scale and micro-scale (global travel, inter-species contagion, protein–protein interactions)."[2] In light of this ambiguous instability, as well as the increasingly fraught relationship between humans and their environment, the social imaginary is being transformed in ways that intimately affect large swathes of the population.

These imaginal shifts generate an affective overtone, which, when amplified via social discourse, resonates through a massive network of lives at various intensities. And the virus has "gone viral" as well; not only does it permeate our biologically shared reality, it also saturates the mediascape that shapes and blurs our private and political lives. Thus augmented, this event has fostered an emergent vocabulary of tenebrosity, which employs the language of theology and myth to articulate a narrative marked by fearfulness, trauma, and, at times, mystery, yet distances it from its metaphysical context(s).

There is the dull darkness of the op-ed stock metaphor—"How to find your silver lining in dark times!"—and the infinitely deeper darkness that seeps from the spectral images of institutional failure and precarity that both haunt and escape visual representation, a shadow under which every glint of sheen disappears. But a more nuanced "stygian symbology" is also emerging that cuts across spectrums of cultural criticism and frames this moment within the mythic imagery of darkness and abyss. Three examples illustrate the richness of this symbology.

A symbology of shadow

In his March *Urbi et Orbi,* Pope Francis evoked biblical epiphany in his contention that a "[t]hick darkness has gathered over our squares, our streets and our cities, "which" fill[s] everything with a… distressing void."[3] Ideologically distant, yet close in tone, Slavoj Žižek contends that the virus is a "dark shadow," which reveals "the ultimate abyss of our being" and plagues Western consciousness, as if it were one of the "undead"—images that thread together Christian symbolism, psychoanalytic parlance, and hauntological imagery.[4] Timothy Morton, the aforementioned proponent of "dark ecology," imagines the pandemic in terms that both buttress and "make strange" the material(ist) horizons of the situation. For Morton, the virus is a "hyperobject," an object so massively distributed in spacetime that it challenges our understanding of objecthood, which grimly announces the greater hyperobject of climate change; it also heralds the arrival of an ambiguous "goddess" who reveals an immanentist nondualism antithetical to Western patriarchal metaphysics.[5]

Pope Francis' "thick darkness" evokes spiritual calamity and the obscurity of the hidden God, threading this embattled moment into a larger metaphysics; Žižek's darkness is functionally nihilistic—"the virus hides no deeper meaning"—and yet he speculates that it may catalyze novel forms of enlightened communism;[6] for Morton, the virus is an epiphenomenon of an all-consuming ecological crisis, a darkness that is equal parts "dark-depressing" (we are complicit in this inescapable crisis), "dark-uncanny" (self and world become strange as distinctions between human and other-than-human worlds dissolve), and strangely "dark-sweet" (new ways of "being ecological" may emerge).[7]

Given the ecological implications of the crisis, it is fitting that darkness, a hybrid phenomenon—indexed to environmental, sociopolitical, aesthetic, and religious registers—has been galvanized within the Western social imaginary. And there is something ethically significant about these evocations of darkness: despite representing opposing ideological commitments, the shadowy symbology invoked by Pope Francis, Žižek, and Morton challenges us to radically rethink our relationships to others, ourselves, and the environment; in such dark times, there can be no "business as usual."

Intuitively, this symbology makes sense. From the separation of light and darkness recounted in Genesis 1:4, to Plato's promise of enlightenment from a world of shadows, the binary of light/dark animates many of the West's sacred stories. Moreover, these metaphorics conceal an implicit metaphysics. Light signifies knowledge, morality, productivity, and other commodities; darkness is sinister, light's *other*. This translation of natural phenomena into the cultural currency of metaphorical and metaphysical narratives conceals a subtle politicization of nature and naturalization of political ideologies, which has also shaped discourses on race, gender, and colonialism. Understood through this filter, as a recent Reuters column has it, "the coronavirus is the dark side of a highly productive, urbanized, interconnected and increasingly prosperous world."[8]

A primal image of chaos that collapses the distance between metaphor and metaphysics within a historically nyctophobic—and as Catherine Keller argues, "tehomophobic"—culture, darkness speaks to the radical blurring of the existential and ecological that the current crisis portends.[9] The language of darkness militates against teleological notions of reaching the light at the end of the tunnel as quickly as possible. It also rejects the triumphalist rhetoric that frames the experience of the pandemic in terms of waging, as the White House would have it, "total war on [an] invisible enemy" who will be "conquered" by "innovation and sheer will power,"[10] as well as the quasi-holistic (and necropolitical) logic of sacrifice for a greater good, as in Lieutenant Governor of Texas Dan Patrick's contention that Americans should be ready to give their lives for the sake of the economy, in order to keep "the America that all America loves for [our] children and grandchildren."[11]

Because of the fact that the virus exploits the efficiency of the neoliberal world order, short-term responses have focused on fighting the crisis by containment and armament. And naturally the situation demands protective withdrawal on personal levels as well. Paradoxically, however, if long-term changes are to be made, the ecological

Viral visions and dark dreams 7

reality revealed by the pandemic—the interdependence of all life laid bare—calls for new practices of imagining openness, of learning how to be affected. What then might be gained by employing darkness as a lens? Might there be historical resources for staying with this present darkness long enough to adjust our eyes to a different ecological vision?

My chapter focuses on an iteration of apophatic mysticism that both resonates with, and challenges, contemporary discourses on darkness. I explore this counter-discourse in two exemplary sites, wherein a focus on darkness links up with concern for "the ecological," namely Theodore Roethke's 1960 poem, "In a Dark Time," and Jacob Böhme's (1575–1624) ecopoetic vision of the *Quellgeister*. I argue that Böhme places the apophatic tradition in conversation with Western esotericism and early modern *Naturmystik*, in ways that effectively transpose it into an ecological key. I trace an emergent "existential ecology" that envisions humans and nature as nonquantifiable phenomena, advocates for a reciprocal relationship between them, and prioritizes embodied experience—in short: *a mode of being that resonates with the radically enmeshed vision of reality unveiled by the virus.* In closing, I suggest that this heterodox intersection of apophatic mysticism and Western esotericism offers resources for a hermeneutics of darkness that challenges the technophiliac logic of late capitalism and offers resources for forging a countercultural mode of perception and an ethics of affect.

Tenebrous temporality

Theodore Roethke's haunting poem "In a Dark Time" begins with the evocative stanzas:

> In a dark time, the eye begins to see,
> I meet my shadow in the deepening shade;
> I hear my echo in the echoing wood—
> A lord of nature weeping to a tree.[12]

Here, the poet encounters a natural environment become strange; the resonance of his own doubled self calls back from within a shifting landscape. As signal and echo blur into confusion, the poet is granted a paradoxical mode of sight, rooted in darkness rather than light—*a vision more visceral than visual*. While composing the poem Roethke was, by his own admission, "in deep therapy…really scraping bedrock."[13] Yet "the deepening shade" is a harbinger of more than depression; the dark time is also the time of the "echoing wood," a distended moment that shelters a "night flowing with birds, a ragged moon."[14]

If we take the poet at his word, this haunted, echoic vision of nature should not be read in a purely figurative manner; its mode of reality is ontologically unstable, metaxic: "both literal *and* symbolic."[15] This instability reverberates with one of Roethke's inspirations, William Blake, who contended, "to the eyes of the man of imagination, nature is imagination itself."[16] Sounded in an idealist key, this statement seemingly reduces the natural world to the imaginal projection of the visionary subject; however, this ignores Blake's refusal to envision the imagination as a subjective, privatized capacity. Read ecologically, both Blake and Roethke underscore the consubstantiality of the human and other-than-human world(s) by underscoring at once the material nature of the imagination, and the nonphenomenalizable dimension of the natural world; paradoxically then, here the imagination names the fluidity between the human and other-than-human worlds, rather than the poet's ability to fix the world within images.

True to the perspective of the porous subject that inhabits the dark time, the poet speaks from *within* the other-than-human world in a manner geometric metaphors cannot map. The tree that receives his tears is not an object grasped by a subject; it is "a growing thing" he can "touch and feel."[17] More radically, the aerial and chthonic creatures that inhabit the poem's latter stanzas are loosed from the weight of symbology as they interpenetrate the poet's very being: "I partake of them all-heron and wren, beast and serpent. They surround me; they protect me; they are my nearest and dearest neighbors."[18]

In the final lines, another type of darkness looms. Rather than searching for a light within or beyond the darkness, the poet takes the darkness *as* a light, a sensual knowledge bound up with shadowy *erôs*:

Dark, dark my light, and darker my desire.[19]

The poem closes with an evocation of mystical union:

The mind enters itself, and God the mind,
And one is One, free in the tearing wind.[20]

This is the divine darkness of apophatic or via negativa mysticism, a tradition seeded in the Platonic notion of "beyond being" (*epekeina tes ousias*),[21] galvanized by Pseudo-Dionysius (ca. fifth/sixth CE), and reimagined by Meister Eckhart, St. John of the Cross, and Jacob Böhme, among others.[22] Like Roethke's shadowy epiphany, apophaticism eschews the luminous language of positivism in its devotion to darkness; it speaks paradoxically of the ineffability of its subject and fosters a unique constellation of ontological and epistemological positions.

Pseudo-Dionysius' work theopoeticized the absolute as divine darkness: the traceless trace of a Godhead too wild to be caged by intellection or sensation. The mode of un/knowing proper to Dionysian apophaticism is not luminous certainty, but the gloom of *agnosia*—an experiential revelation of shadow rather than a detached vision of light.[23] The initiate moves from the worlds of sensual and intellectual intelligibility into "the brilliant darkness of a hidden silence."[24] Roethke's poem however does not transcend the sensual realm; even in its confrontation with the divine darkness, the poem winds back in echoic reflection toward a haunted, living nature, before coiling into the poet's own desire. Within this dark dream, the contour of an existential darkness emerges that reverberates with an "ecological darkness": a blurring of the divide between human and other-than-human worlds. This ecological darkness opens up to the transcendental darkness of an existence beyond the reach of concept or category. Yet, neither poet nor nature disappears in this triangulation; rather, a shifting place opens that shelters an "ecological subject," a sense of self shot through with *otherness*, enmeshed with the elemental and the animal.

Eco-erotic enmeshment

The heterodox mystic Jacob Böhme (1575–1624) weaves his image of human being from a similar mesh of existential, ecological, and divine darknesses. Böhme conjoins the apophatic tradition with Paracelsian *Naturmystik* filtered through an existentialized vision of alchemy. While eschewing systematization, Böhme develops a complex, mythopoetic anthropology that prioritizes affect and existential openness. Unlike his contemporary Descartes, Böhme does not ground the self within the act of cognition; ipseity is envisioned as an epiphenomenon of "desire" (*Begehren*), which is the soul's dark root.[25] Thus, although Böhme's work is often referred to as "visionary," this term should be qualified; as with Roethke's dark time, here we find an imaginary drawn from the invisible realm of bodily sensation and tending toward an unfathomable depth. This limit and source is the "Ungrund" (*Ungrund*), a primordial, erotic "ungroundedness" that enables the paradoxical phenomenon of a beginning that never recedes into the distance of the past:

> The *Ungrund* is an eternal nothing; yet it creates an eternal beginning, which is its craving—for the nothing is a craving after something.[26]

Blurring ontological and epistemological registers, the privative *un* places this term in an antonymic relationship to ground (*Grund*) in the sense of "reason" (*logos*), "foundation," and "cause." A hyper-darkness beyond duality that inheres to, and perpetually destabilizes, divinity, nature, and selfhood, the inner life of the *Ungrund* is presented via Trinitarian imagery as a triple knot of tenebrosity:

> [W]e find that the three are from eternity an unbeginning and unending band of longing, wanting, and desiring. One gives birth to the other. And if one did not exist, neither would the other... no one knows what this band is; in itself it is nothing but a spirit in darkness. And yet, it is not darkness, but rather a nothing, neither darkness nor light.[27]

Far from an abstract concept, *Ungrund* is the outgrowth of an imaginary geared toward transformation rather than predication. Through a practice of spiritual alchemy replete with meditational and somatic exercises, Böhme and his followers strove to be affected by this darkness. Böhme envisions this process of "self-ungrounding" as the growth of a subtle "power-body" (*Kraft-Leib*) from "inner flesh" (*innere Fleisch*).[28] In what follows, I sketch out Böhme's explication of this ungrounded state through his teaching of the "source-spirits" (*Quellgeister*).

The *Quellgeister* stands as one of Böhme's most difficult concepts. Böhme's use of *Quell* semantically intertwines notions of origin, quale/quality, and suffering. Pathos is presented as the primordial condition for the emergence of existence, a process that can be epiphenomenally extricated into seven interpenetrating "spirits" (*Geister*), "forms" (*Gestalten*), or "qualities" (*Qualitäten*). Through the interaction of these seven spirits—an enumeration that draws together alchemical, astrological, and apocalyptic imagery—"all things have been made and have arisen."[29]

Although the spirits can be viewed as distinct forces, they continuously merge into one another, blurring the boundaries of individuality. Their existence, and thus *the fabric of existence as such*, is interdependent, enmeshed:

> ... one spirit cannot generate another by itself; nor can two do so... the birth of a spirit resides in the interaction of all seven spirits... if it were not for one, neither would there be the other.[30]

Although not metaphysically transcendent, neither the temporality nor their spatiality of the spirits can be quantified through geometric coordinates; they evoke a thoroughly anti-mechanistic vision of nature. Through these enmeshed images, an "ecological ontology" appears: a vision wherein being arises, not from a single source or cause, but rather within an ever-shifting field of interrelations. In a striking parallel to the Buddhist notion of "dependent origination" (*Pratītyasamutpāda*), the phenomena and entities that make up existence are presented as inter-reliant and unquantifiable. Although linguistic convention forces Böhme to describe discrete "spirits" that precede or succeed one another, this is illusory:

> All seven... are born within each other; each perpetually gives birth to the other. None is the first, nor is any the last, for the last generates the first just as the first does the second, third, fourth, and so on... for all seven are equally eternal and have neither beginning nor end... and none... exists without the other.[31]

Böhme evokes the interwoven life of the *Quellgeister* in animistic and erotic terms:

> One spirit sees the other... one tastes the other, whereupon they come alive and the power of life penetrates everything. And in that power, one smells the other, and by this surging and penetrating one feels the other, and there is nothing other than a pure, affectionate loving and amiable seeing, pleasant smelling, good tasting, and love feeling, a blissful kissing, eating of one another, drinking and love strolling.[32]

As with *Ungrund*, the *Geister* are not precise philosophical concepts—the smudged edges of these images are integral to their content. Böhme is in fact not entirely consistent in the names or order he assigns to them; there are recurrent patterns, but his impressionistic approach speaks to their unquantifiable nature. One of Böhme's clearest articulations of the sevenfold schema names these "forms of the mother of all being" (*Gestalten der Mutter aller Wesen*) as (1) desire, (2) bitterness, (3) angst, (4) fire, (5) light, (6) sound, and (7) *Corpus* or *Menstruum*.[33]

Read linearly, the *Quellgeister* map a movement from "desire" to "embodiment" (*Corpus*). Yet, consonant with Böhme's subversion of "chronologic," body is said to be the "seed" (*der Same*) of "all these forms"—the origin as well as the consequence of desire. Thus, while *Corpus* appears as the concretization of the spirits, it is also their origin: "flesh is the mother of spirit."[34] The seven not only plot the coordinates of an interdependent ontology, they re-embody and thus *ecologize* existence, grounding selfhood in preconceptual sensation and openness to alterity. The *Quellgeister* map the world via sensation rather than geometric abstraction; they militate against the hierarchical separation of human and other-than-human worlds, subjectivity and objectivity.

At heart, both the "outer" world of nature and the "inner" world of human being blur into dark potentiality of *Ungrund*. Following the logic of the *Quellgeister*, discrete categorization of reality is rendered nonsensical; if worlds arise from interdependent tangles of sensation, it follows that they are intimately entwined with—and inseparable from—sensing subjects. Yet, this very subject arises through the dynamics of encounter. Humans do not stand over and against an already existent world; states such as "desire," "bitterness," or "angst" are ontologically "prior to" all dichotomies, and thus sensual experience marks the event in which subject and object emerge from an abyss of indeterminacy.

The *Quellgeister* comprise what could be called a "double-flesh," formally akin to Merleau-Ponty's notion of *la chair* ("the flesh").[35] Though contextualized by different operational assumptions, here, as with Merleau-Ponty, "the thickness of the body" is presented as the "sole means" of going "unto the heart of the things" by making the self "a world" and the world "flesh."[36] But, like Roethke's echoing wood, this flesh is doubled: the *Quellgeister* allow for the interpenetration and reversibility of world and body-self. The world of the body and the body of the world open up to one another, they "belong…to one sole space of consciousness."[37]

By positing as primary principles what would traditionally be interpreted as either secondary qualities—"bitterness" and "sound"—or psychosomatic states—"desire" and "angst"—Böhme begins with nodes of interdependent origination, "touch points" that privilege neither the physical nor the mental. Both sensation and affect, the spirits simultaneously prefigure and give birth to both sensing subject and sensed object. Mapping an *eco-erotic poetics*, a language capable of expressing an awareness of self and world prior to the threshold of detached reflection, the double-flesh firmly roots humans within the world and the world within humans, while sheltering the darkness of *Ungrund*. Akin to Roethke's vision, the Böhmean subject is not the measure of all things, but their *threshold*. Actualizing ungroundedness does not entail transcending body or nature; rather, one should exist *in media res* with attuned awareness: "one's consciousness need not pass out of this world, it finds everything in this world, there in itself, and indeed in all that lives and moves."[38]

Does the dark, too, bloom and sing?

Like Roethke, we too find ourselves in a dark time, confronted by a crisis so massive it exceeds our powers of conception and appears only epiphenomenally. Within this darkness, we are haunted by the threat of

Viral visions and dark dreams 13

a double blindness, at once ethical and epistemological. The pandemic has demanded novel forms of technocratic protection and control to be implemented. But this is not enough. In the wake of COVID-19, it has become impossible to ignore the extreme injustices that have resulted from the ways that we have curated and imagined our hyper-networked world. The virus reveals myriad ecological and existential emergencies that constellate around an overarching crisis of relationality, which in turn threads together environmental, economic, and social justice issues.[39]

If the sociocultural changes we make are to be more than technocratically enforced fortifications, it is crucial that, as Lynn White's seminal essay on the ecological crisis argues, we must not only "rethink" but also "refeel our nature and destiny."[40] Alongside employing Enlightenment-based forms of thought, it is necessary to confront the shadow side of the situation. It is not sufficient to only effect change, but we must also learn how to *be affected* in new ways that respond to the reality of our radical enmeshment.

In "How to Talk about the Body?" Bruno Latour writes of embodiment as a "learning to be affected"—a concept he illustrates by referencing the French perfume industry's use of "odor kits" (*malette à odeurs*) to train aspiring perfumists.[41] Latour points out that the perfumist does not simply acquire new information in the form of data. The term "sense" names a phenomenon neither entirely dependent upon the sensing subject or the sensed object, but co-constituted through interaction; aspirants train to be affected in new ways and thus extend and augment their own sensual bodies. *Mutatis mutandis*, Latour's theory of embodiment resonates with Roethke and Böhme's existential ecopoetics: "acquiring a body is thus a progressive enterprise that produces at once a sensory medium and a sensitive world."[42]

Part of the task of forging a new eco-ethics that honors human and other-than-human interdependence and reflects our shared precarity is imagining new modes of embodiment, individually and socially. As Jane Bennett points out, "affect is central to politics and ethics."[43] If, in the face of the sociopolitical, economic, and existential regimes that have moved us toward a state of ecological crisis, we are to catalyze lasting transformation, new practices of imagining and becoming *otherwise* will have to be developed. And it is in fashioning a new "counter culture of perceiving," able to adjust its eyes to these dark times, that many of the vocations devalued under the aegis of neoliberalism—artists, philosophers, theologians, and poets—have crucial roles to play.[44] Here, outside of institutionalism, a decentered, patchwork conversation has the chance to be seeded.

Echoes of inspiration might be heard within Böhme's heterodox thought and its reverberance in the visionary-poetic tradition that could supply raw materials toward a new heterodoxy—one that challenges the values of technophiliac free market capitalism. As Federico Campagna argues, we must use what historical resources we have to reclaim the possibility of "[a] world open to a radical 'elsewhere' both within and without…[a] world we know in our hearts, yet are told by Technic's regime to be impossible and mere superstition."[45] To be clear, I am not suggesting a "return to" a premodern state of enchantment—whatever that might mean—rather, as we forge ahead into the darkness, I contend that a creative reexamination of traces of thought and practice that lie on the margins of the West's self-narrativization would be fruitful; there in the historical dustbins of "rejected knowledge," we might find forms of thought that lead elsewhere than the path we are on.[46] In this context, the apophatic tradition is rich with an imaginary that has much to say outside of its historical contexts. This may sound like a tenuous approach to such a cataclysmic moment; but part of what needs to be felt in dark times is the tenuous nature of reality. Thus, to borrow the words of Wendell Berry, if we accustom our eyes to the present darkness and stay with it long enough to dream otherwise, we may "find that the dark, too, blooms and sings."[47]

Notes

1 Timothy Morton, "The Mesh," in Stephanie LeMenager, Teresa Shewry, and Ken Hiltner, eds., *Environmental Criticism for the Twenty-First Century* (New York: Routledge, 2011), 24. On "ecognosis" see Timothy Morton, *Dark Ecology: For a Logic of Future Coexistence* (New York: Columbia University Press, 2016), 5–6.
2 Eugene Thacker, "The Shadows of Atheology: Epidemics, Power and Life after Foucault," *Theory, Culture & Society* (SAGE, Los Angeles, London, New Delhi, and Singapore) 26(6) (2009): 134–152, 135.
3 The address was given on Saturday, March 28th, 2020. http://w2.vatican.va/content/francesco/en/messages/urbi/documents/papa-francesco_20200327_urbi-et-orbi-epidemia.html.
4 Slavoj Žižek, *Pandemic! COVID-19 Shakes the World* (Cambridge: Polity Press, 2020), 52, 134.
5 Timothy Morton interviewed for the STRP Festival (online). https://strp.nl/program/timothy-morton.
6 Žižek, *Pandemic*, 14, 95–106.
7 Morton, *Dark Ecology*, 5.
8 John Kemp, "Column: Coronavirus Is Dark Side of an Urban Interconnected World," https://www.reuters.com/article/us-global-energy-kemp/column-coronavirus-is-dark-side-of-an-urban-interconnected-world-kemp-idUSKBN22Y17I.

Viral visions and dark dreams 15

9 The term references the Hebrew word "tehom" in Genesis 1:2, "abyss." Catherine Keller, *Face of the Deep: A Theology of Becoming* (New York: Routledge, 2003), 23–32.
10 Form letter from the White House regarding the economic impact payment, May 8, 2020.
11 The statement occurred on Fox News on March 23 as Patrick was interviewed by Tucker Carlson. For an introduction to "necropolitics," see J.A. Mbembé and Libby Meintjes, *Public Culture* 15(1) (Winter 2003): 11–40.
12 Theodore Roethke, *Selected Poems* (Library of America; First Edition: no city given, 2005), 116, lines 1–4.
13 Theodore Roethke, *Selected Letters of Theodore Roethke* (Seattle: University of Washington Press, 1968), 218.
14 Roethke, *Selected Poems*, line 14.
15 Anthony Ostroff, ed., *The Contemporary Poet as Artist and Critic* (Boston, MA: Little, Brown, 1964), 50. Italics mine.
16 William Blake, "Letter to Revd Tusler, August 23, 1799," in David Erdman, ed., *The Complete Poetry of William Blake* (Berkeley: University of California Press, 2008), 702.
17 Ralph J. Mills, Jr., ed., *Selected Letters of Theodore Roethke* (Seattle: University of Washington Press, 1968), 218.
18 Ibid. 50.
19 Roethke, *Selected Poems*, 116, line 19.
20 Ibid. lines 23–24.
21 Plato, *Republic*, 509b, 6.590b.
22 "Apophatic" stems from *apophanai*, "to speak off or away from," implying the paradox of speaking the unspeakable. See: Denys Turner, *The Darkness of God: Negativity in Christian Mysticism* (Cambridge: Cambridge University Press, 1995).
23 Pseudo-Dionysius, *Mystical Theology*, 1.3 1001A; CD II 144.10–15.
24 Ibid. 997AB.
25 Jacob Böhme, *Das Ugewandte Auge*, IV 7, 180. All Böhme quotations are taken from the *Sämtliche Schriften*, ed., Will-Eric Peuckert (Stuttgart: Günter Holzboog, 1956–1960). Translations are mine. Renderings of passages from *Morgenröthe im Aufgang* benefited from consulting Andrew Week's excellent translation in Jakob Böhme, *Aurora: (Morgen Röte im auffgang, 1612) and Ein gründlicher Bericht or A Fundamental Report (Mysterium Pansophicum, 1620)*, transl. Andrew Weeks, (Leiden: Brill, 2013).
26 Böhme, *Von der Menschwerdung Jesu Christi*, VII 3. Teil 5, 5, 10.
27 Böhme, *Von den drey Principien*, II 14: 62, 184–185. The term *das vnanfengig* stems from Paracelsus.
28 Böhme, *Vierzig Fragen von der Seele*. IV 7: 17, 76, IV1: 42, 165.
29 Böhme, *Morgenröthe im Aufgang* I 9: 41, 111. See also: Andrew Weeks, *Boehme: An Intellectual Biography* (Albany, NY: SUNY Press, 1991), 73–75.
30 Ibid. 10: 21, 117–118.
31 Ibid. 10: 2, 114.
32 Ibid. 9: 37–39, 110–111.
33 This version of the "Quellgeister" is taken from Böhme, *Von der Geburt und Bezeichnung aller Wesen*, XIV 14: 10–11, 196–197. C.F. Böhme, *Erklärung*

der Vornehmsten Puncten und Wörter in diesen Schriften. XX 8–9: 25–80, 85–96.
34 Böhme, *Morgenröthe im Aufgang*, I 21: 69, 310.
35 Maurice Merleau-Ponty, *The Visible and the Invisible*, transl. Alphonso Lingus (Evanston, IL: Northwestern University Press, 1968), 130–155.
36 Ibid. 135.
37 Ibid. 141.
38 Böhme, *Beschreibung der Drey Principien Göttliches Wesen*, II 8: 1, 73.
39 As I finish this chapter, demonstrations have erupted in the United States to protest systemic racism and police brutality, which bring another dimension of the crisis to light. Unfortunately, I do not have the space to address this crucial aspect here; I would simply like to note that COVID-19 has foregrounded the enmeshment of social-ecological and environmental crises.
40 Lynn White, "The Historical Roots of Our Ecological Crisis," *Science*, New Series 155(3767) (March 10, 1967): 1207.
41 Bruno Latour, "How to Talk about the Body? The Normative Dimensions of Science Studies," *Body & Science* 10(2–3) (2004): 207–212.
42 Ibid. 207.
43 Jane Bennett, *Vibrant Matter: A Political Ecology of Things* (Durham, NC: Duke University Press, 2010), xxi.
44 Ibid. xiv.
45 Federico Campagna, *Technic and Magic: The Reconstruction of Reality* (London: Bloomsbury Academic, 2018), 49.
46 I borrow the phrase from Wouter Hanegraaff's *Esotericism and the Academy: Rejected Knowledge in Western Culture* (Cambridge: Cambridge University Press), 2012.
47 Wendell Berry, *The Selected Poems of Wendell Berry* (Washington, DC: Counterpoint, 1998), 68.

2 Ecology and the unbuffered self
Identity, agency, and authority in a time of pandemic

Alexander J. B. Hampton

The pandemic crisis significantly challenges the modern social imaginary, the pre-reflective, tacit, paradigmatic stories, images, and ideologies by which we conceptualise ourselves and our place in the world. It does this in a way that no other natural phenomenon—not species extinction, nor air pollution, nor climate change—has. It forces human beings to re-think what Charles Taylor has aptly described as the buffered self, shared by most inhabitants of the globalised and industrialised world.[1] This buffered self, the paradigm of the modern social imaginary, has given us profound powers to reshape nature, whilst simultaneously disconnecting us from it, with devastating consequences. Such civilisational disconnect can only be overcome by an epochal shift in the modern social imaginary which we occupy, of the kind we might presently be experiencing in the pandemic. The historian Peter Hennessy conveyed the significance of the pandemic when he stated that future historians would divide our age into BC and AC, 'Before corona, and after corona'.[2]

This consideration aims to characterise the crisis and opportunity of COVID-19 in three parts: first, it will set out the problematic conceptualisation of nature in the modern social imaginary by focusing upon the buffered self in terms of its sense of identity, agency, and authority. Second, it will set out how the pandemic fundamentally disrupts these three facets of the buffered self in terms of the fragilisation of economic values, the notion of unique human agency, and the limitation of the authority of discursive reason. Finally, it will conclude by outlining the opportunity for a renewed relationship with nature by proposing the recovery of premodern concepts structurally excluded from the modern social imaginary, not as simple forms of re-enchantment, but as resources for creatively re-thinking nature and our place within it. In particular, it will consider the notions of the metaphysics of participation, the concept of teleology, and the concept of rational intuition. Here, in a moment of global grief and disruption, and in the face of fundamental challenges that un-buffer the modern self, we are presented with an opportunity, not just to solve the acute crisis of the pandemic, but to address the ecological crisis of the modern age by rethinking our collective concept of nature, and the place of our now un-buffered selves within it.

The modern buffered self

The process by which we came to be modern buffered selves is a long and complex one, far beyond the scope of an examination of this size.[3] However, we can come to a brief characterisation of it by identifying three key facets that define and differentiate it from the premodern self from which it emerged, namely its unique sense of identity, agency, and authority. In doing so, the aim is not to highlight a favourable premodern understanding over a problematic modern one. Rather, it is to illustrate that the modern buffered self developed along with a concurrent structural exclusion of specific ways of thinking, which deeply influence humanity's collective connection to non-human reality.[4]

Identity

For the buffered self, identity is grounded in self-originating concepts of meaning and value, whether originating in one's own self, or other autonomous selves. The modern self therefore is established in the context of a subject-object dynamic, where individual subjects and their internal concepts are set over and against external objects, creating the framework for the modern sense of autonomy.[5] Alternatively, for the premodern self, identity is manifested through a relational framework, where meaning and value are intelligible ontic realities, adhering both in the external corporal realities that instantiate them, and in the internal mental thoughts of the mind that think them. The result is a heteronymic notion of agency, based upon an interdependent subject-object dialogue, where meaning and value are determined dialogically.

The difference between the modern and the premodern is exemplified by comparing Aquinas and Kant on the concept of ideas.[6] In Aquinas' realist, participatory metaphysics we find a succinct formulation: 'by ideas are understood the forms of things, existing apart from the things themselves... [either as] the type of that which is called the form, or to be the principle of the knowledge of that thing'.[7] Contrastingly, in the critical idealist philosophy of Kant, we find an opposing formulation: 'The idea is a concept of reason whose object can be met with nowhere in experience'.[8] What is expressed here by idealism is also true for many other modern positions, be it Cartesian rationalism, Lockean empiricism, or linguistic structuralism, viz. the position that there is no knowledge of external reality except through its internal representation.[9]

The modern construction of autonomous identity leaves the external world, and particularly the natural world, devoid of inherent meaning and value. Rather, external reality becomes the raw material to which anthropocentric meaning and value is applied. Autonomous modern identity bases itself on its powerful capacity to confer meaning as part of its own process of self-determination. In this context the natural world becomes an unprocessed resource of fungible, identikit materials awaiting human exploitation.[10]

Agency

Agency for the buffered self is conceptualised in a similar way, as an exclusively human capacity. It is only humans who are capable of acting upon a purpose, with intentionality, towards an end. Purposes, or ends, are something that are added to nature externally, either by humans, or in some modern conceptualisations by God as the artificer of the mechanism of creation.[11] This may be contrasted to premodern understanding, where non-exclusive human agency is situated within a network of interlocking agencies, both human and non-human, deliberative and non-deliberative. For the premodern intellectual framework, God did not create a mechanism and set it to run; rather creatures are sustained by God's continuation of existence.[12] In the case of divine involvement, what individual creatures have from God's agency, they truly have themselves as their own, whilst also having that agency only from God.

Again, we can exemplify this by contrasting modern and premodern understandings of Aristotelian causation. For example, Averroes defends the attribution of agency to non-human objects, such as fire, whether they act voluntarily or non-voluntarily: 'an agent [$fā'il$] is what causes some other thing to pass from potency to actuality and from non-existence to existence; this actualization occurs sometimes from deliberation and choice, sometimes by nature'.[13] Compare this to Bacon, who argues:

> It is rightly laid down that true knowledge is that which is deduced from causes. The division of four causes also is not amiss: matter,

form, the efficient, and end or final cause. Of these, however, the latter is so far from being beneficial, that it even corrupts the sciences, except in the intercourse of man with man.[14]

For Bacon, the agency of final cause is only useful in the explanation of human actions, as only humans are capable of determining purpose, and acting with intent. For non-human nature, the attribution of agency only undermines our understanding of its operation.

Again, there are consequences. The modern anthropocentric conceptualisation of agency withdraws any agency from nature. The external world is left to be understood in the passive, mechanical terms of cause and effect. This leaves nature as a blind mechanism, either created by a watchmaker God or directionless, as is the case with natural selection. The result is that there is no external agency with which the modern self must negotiate, with the exception of other selves. Instead, agency is something which is added to a passive, mechanistic nature, by either God or humans, who give it purpose.

Authority

The final facet of the buffered self to consider is its authority. Through its sense of autonomous identity and unique agency, the buffered self is capable of distancing itself from both the physical and psychical self embedded in nature. It does this through the reconstruction of external reality according to the disciplined application of intrinsic categories of discursive reason. This makes it possible to dismiss the physical and emotional as inauthentic and irrational to the true self. The result is that the buffered self gains a sense of invulnerability, based upon the authority of its own objective, self-evident principles. This invulnerability can be distinguished from the premodern self, whose authority is restricted by its vulnerability to extrinsic ideas and non-human agents. External meaning and value elicit intuitive reason, expressed in desire and emotion, to which the self must by necessity respond. Similarly, external agencies, both human and non-human, must be negotiated with or confronted as realities.[15]

An example of the vulnerable premodern self is the Christian Platonism of Pseudo-Dionysius, for whom 'all being derives from, exists in, and is returned toward the Beautiful and the Good', which are divine names for God.[16] All things, human and non-human, animate and inanimate, 'are stirred to do and to will whatever it is they do and will because of their yearning for the Beautiful and the Good', which is at once their divine origin and their divine end.[17] Here, to know the self is to be attuned to the cosmic order, to follow one's intuitive reason, in desire and yearning, and to relate them to the divine end which is their source. By contrast, Descartes offered a position based upon radical doubt that was distrusting of both the senses and tradition, and focused upon that which was possible to know with authority. Rules two and three of his *Rules for the Direction of the Mind* read:

> We should attend only to those objects of which our minds seem capable of having certain and indubitable cognition.
>
> Concerning objects proposed for study, we ought to investigate what we can clearly and evidently intuit or deduce with certainty, and not what other people have thought or what we ourselves conjecture. For knowledge can be attained in no other way.[18]

Here, knowledge is restricted to the ordered representation of reality, distanced from the deceiving senses and emotional conjecture, and derives its authority from the disciplined deliberation of the autonomous self.

The authority that the buffered self derives from this reconstruction of external reality profoundly affects the ways we conceive of nature and our place within it. Our physical disembedding is recapitulated through the abstract values and meaning which are used to reconstruct it, either through intellectual systems, such as the sciences and economics, or in the construction of the Cartesian grid cities which the modern social imaginary imposes upon the landscapes that our buffered selves occupy. Similarly, our psychic reactions to nature, whether manifest as a desire to be part of it, or the sense of intrinsic value and meaning derived from its beauty and goodness, are delegitimated as sentimentality, or epiphenomenal remnants of a primitive past.

Pandemic and un-buffering the self

The pandemic presents a situation that fundamentally challenges the modern social imaginary. In particular, it undermines the three facets of the buffered self as elaborated above, and in so doing, the way we conceptualise the human-nature relationship.

Identity

First, the pandemic disrupts the buffered self's self-originating construction of meaning and value, and in so doing challenges the autonomous identity upon which it is based. This is particularly manifested in the fragilisation of economic meaning and value, arguably the most powerful meaning-value system in operation in the modern social imaginary. For example, this is evinced in national GDP projections that predict 2020 declines ranging from −2.8% to more than −15% depending upon the country, modelling methodology, and the length of local public health measures.[19] This in turn effects identity formation, as the modern social imaginary constructs self identity by determining actions, motivations, and forms of self-definition within the matrix of capital. Yet in the face of the pandemic such self-defining activities have been destabilised, particularly in terms of education and employment.[20] Adding to this, the collapse of the value of numerous commodities and economic activities generates uncertainties that affect human well-being on a wide socio-psychological scale.[21] Finally, challenges to the economic meaning-value system, which in diverse ways encompass nations and transcend political orientations, undermine the sacrosanct principles of identity-forming political ideologies, from the confidence of some in the efficacy of centralised state direction and provision, to the belief of others in the efficiency and wealth re-distributing powers of economic globalisation.[22]

Agency

Second, the notion of unique human agency is undermined. In one manner, the pandemic reveals an entangled network of human and non-human agencies that impinges upon the free activity of exclusive human agency. Such impingements are not rare occurrences; however in almost all occasions they are rendered localisable or imperceptible within the broad framework of the modern social imaginary, thereby allowing them to be subsumed into a system that denies their agency based upon the anthropocentric notion of individual intentionality. Even such continent-wide events as the Australian brush fires of 2019–2020, or the mass famine in West Africa caused by the 2012 Sahel drought, despite their scale, can still be rendered distant, and therefore not a consequence of the wider disconnect between agency conceived anthropocentrically and its broader actuality.[23] Yet, whilst these probable symptoms of climate change can be localised, the pandemic affects human agency on an immediate, visceral and global scale that cannot be subsumed into the modern social imaginary.

In another manner, the pandemic exposes the normalised injustice of the unequal actualisation of agency among human actors, laid bare in the disproportionate suffering of marginalised individuals and groups. Examples such as state coercion and oppression in communist China, or economic and political disenfranchisement in the United

States, are brought into greater relief.[24] Both are transverse manifestations of an understanding of human agency determined anthropocentrically and conceived in terms of economic meaning and value that benefits a select group, rather than extrinsically determined meaning and value, conceived in the context of a network of interlocking agencies, both human and non-human.

Authority

Finally, the authority of the buffered self, based upon the reconstruction of nature through invulnerable discursive reason, shows its limitations in the context of the pandemic. Well before COVID-19, virologists were warning about the limitations of an abstract definition of life which requires the exclusion of viruses.[25] A consequence of this exclusion is that biological experiments are often conducted in artificial and unrealistic conditions that exclude the role of viruses.[26] This abstract re-construction of nature results in unintended negative consequences for the understanding of life in general, the role of viruses in particular, and the practical ability to consider and manage their effects. In this way, the pandemic demonstrates the limitations of authoritative discursive reason, which in this instance has failed to take account of the virosphere in which all life operates because of the limitations of the abstract framework it imposes upon nature.

Simultaneously, whilst the invulnerability of the detached self is undermined, its emotive entanglements with the natural world are revealed as far from overcome. The pandemic has brought emotions to the fore of our collective conscious actions. This has been demonstrated by panic consumption and xenophobia, which were among the first reactions to overcome the emotional and physical detachment of the buffered self. However, it has also surprisingly manifested itself in joy and wonderment, in the form of a renewed connection to nature. Among the second wave of stories following the initial period of pandemic panic were media reports from urban areas around the world of once again hearing birdsong, and of seeing wildlife in places from which it had previously been excluded or its presence obscured.[27] Though such stories can convey a problematic anthropocentric self-congratulatory element, this human awareness of non-human meaning and value, in the context of pandemic-limited human agency, also invites humans back into dialogue with the natural world which we, in our modern social imaginary, have buffered ourselves from.[28]

Apocalypse and opportunity

The word apocalypse (*apo*: 'off', and *kaluptein*: 'to cover') tends to be invoked as a synonym for cataclysm, yet the accurate theological use of the term, to uncover or unveil something, is remarkably accurate to the situation. In the midst of challenge and grief, the pandemic presents the opportunity to escape the mind-forged manacles of the buffered self. This positive apocalypse, in challenging the modern social imaginary, directs our attention back to premodern theological modes of conceptualising the human-nature relationship. These cannot, nor should they be, adopted wholesale into our modern context. However, they do offer themselves as a resource for the present-day challenge of reconceptualising nature and the place of humans within it, in the context of the pandemic un-buffering of the self.

Identity

The pandemic challenge to subject-centred concepts of meaning and value, and to the anthropocentric construction of identity that arises from them, invites us to re-examine the philosophical notions of realism and participation, which understand the external world as possessed of its own meaning and value, and its own intrinsic identities, regardless of a human presence to acknowledge and confirm them. Realism is a philosophical position which holds that ideals (or ideas, forms, transcendentals) are real extra-mental realities that transcend both the objects that instantiate them and the minds that think them. The cosmos participates in these ideas, making the intelligible archetypes corporally present, unfolding them in myriad and unique ways.[29] A realist-participatory view of reality, therefore, requires individuals to conceptualise the natural world as something with which they must dialogue in order to arrive at concepts of meaning and value, rather than imposing these themselves from without. By extension, in the realist context, nature is also something that possesses, and is therefore capable of teaching true, mind-independent meaning and value. It is in the context of this subject-object exchange that human identity can be formed dialogically with the external natural world, possessed of its own identities. The result of realism, therefore, is to render nature no longer a raw material or fungible resource to which meaning and value are added monologically by the self. Rather, nature is a reality, with its own inherent meaning and value, which demands a level of recognition based upon its own intrinsic worth.[30]

Agency

It follows from the notion that all things in the cosmos participate in philosophically real meaning and value, that these real ideals also give all things their own purpose. In the apocalypse (unveiling) of the pandemic, we may begin to appreciate the notion that ends, or teloi, are intrinsic to all creatures themselves, human and non-human, intentional and natural, even animate and inanimate. The pandemic disruption to exclusive human agency reveals a complex ecology of interlocking agents and ends. This recognition of relationality in agency demands of us that we exercise our own agency relationally as well. The concept of teleology teaches us that matter is not merely passive, and purpose is not something imposed from outside; instead, 'every agent acts for an end'.[31] Thus, our own agency is entangled with other agents, and this must be understood as a characteristic of being an agent, not a limitation upon agency. The flourishing of both human and non-human nature is something that can only occur within this understanding of a network of shared, interdependent agencies. Greater cognisance of the multiplicity of agencies will lead us to better account for not only non-human agents, but also fellow humans, as the exercise of agency shifts away from a narrow individualistic perspective, to a wider one which aims to encompass a broad ecology of actors.[32]

Authority

Finally, the apocalyptic uncovering of the pandemic, in throwing the abstract reconstruction of nature by discursive reason into doubt, and overwhelming the physical and psychic disembeddedness of the buffered self, calls for a recovery of our affective relationship to nature. Being in the natural world has long evoked desire, and the intuition 'of something far more deeply interfused', as Wordsworth put it.[33] Building upon the notions of participation and teleology, our intuitive reactions to the natural world ought to be re-evaluated. Intuitive reason, in contrast to apodictic discursive reason, has often been understood as the means to arrive at truths about the world, perceived dimly at first, but in the fullness of time understood more deeply.[34] Rather than understanding the feelings of desire and depth evoked by being in and experiencing nature as projections of the ego, they may be understood as genuine responses to the meaning intrinsic to nature itself, to its identity and its agency. As such, affection allows us to understand something about nature that quantification and abstract generalisation cannot. This points us towards the latent possibility present in the language of aesthetics, developed in harmony with the cadence of nature, to sit alongside the more austere representations yielded by the natural sciences.[35]

In the disruption of the pandemic, and the challenges it poses to the modern social imaginary, there is an opportunity to form a renewed relationship with nature. As the sense of identity, agency, and authority that defines the buffered self is respectively undermined by the fragilisation of economic values, the impingement of extra-human agency, and the limitation of the authority of discursive reason, an apocalyptic opportunity presents itself. Ways of thinking about nature and the place of humans within it that were previously structurally excluded once again become available in the un-buffering of the self. Each of those taken up here—realist participation, theology and non-human agency, and intuitive reason—do not present themselves as simple tools for re-enchantment, but they do offer us resources for creatively re-thinking the human-nature relationship. Whilst a simple return to the premodern is neither possible nor desirable, the un-buffering of the self, and the loosening of the modern social imaginary present the opportunity for the emergence of a set of new hybrid possibilities for conceiving of ourselves in and of nature. These possibilities recognise that nature is possessed of its own agency and ends, and constituted by meanings and values which we must come to know on nature's own terms.

Notes

1 Charles Taylor, *A Secular Age* (Cambridge, MA: Harvard University Press, 2007), 27, 37 42, 131–142, 262–264, 300–307.
2 Lord Peter Hennessey, interview by Sarah Montague, *BBC Radio 4, World at One*, March 14, 2020, at 8:15 mins.
3 A number of historical narratives describe the emergence of modern identity. E.g. Hans Blumenberg, *Die Legitimität der Neuzeit* (Frankfurt a.M.: Suhrkamp, 1966); Charles Taylor, *Sources of the Self* (Cambridge, MA: Harvard University Press, 1989); Charles Taylor, *A Secular Age* (Cambridge, MA: Harvard University Press, 2007); Jerome B. Schneewind, *The Invention of Autonomy* (Cambridge: Cambridge University Press, 1998); Michael Allen Gillespie, *Theological Origins of Modernity* (Chicago, IL: University of Chicago Press. 2008).
4 A similar case can be made for displaced forms of understanding nature offered by other world religions and indigenous religions, displaced by the globalised modern social imaginary and the buffered self.
5 Taylor, *Sources*, 188.
6 Alexander J.B. Hampton, "Transcendence and Immanence: Deciphering Their Relation through the Transcendentals in Aquinas and Kant," *Toronto Journal of Theology* 34, no. 2 (2018), 187–198.
7 Thomas Aquinas, *The Summa Theologiæ of St. Thomas Aquinas*, trans. Fathers of the English Dominican Province (London: Burns, Oates & Washbourne, 1911–1925), Ia.15.1.

8 Immanuel Kant, *Lectures on Logic*, trans. J. Michael Young (Cambridge: Cambridge University Press, 1992), 590.
9 Hubert Dreyfus and Charles Taylor, *Retrieving Realism* (Cambridge, MA: Harvard University Press, 2015), 3.
10 Alexander J.B. Hampton, "Christian Platonism, Nature and Environmental Crisis," in *Christian Platonism: A History* (Cambridge: Cambridge University Press, 2020), 381–407.
11 William Paley, *Natural Theology*, eds. Matthew D. Eddy and David Knight (Oxford: Oxford University Press, 2008), 7–10.
12 *Summa Theologiæ*, Ia.104.1; II *Sent*. 1.1.5 in Thomas Aquinas, *Aquinas on Creation*, trans. Steven E. Baldner and W.E. Carroll (Toronto: Pontifical Institute of Mediaeval Studies, 1997), 102.
13 In this context Averroes is defending the inherent agency in creation against its attribution, as he sees it in Al-Ghazali's emanation philosophy, to God's agency alone. Averroes, *Tahafut al-tahafut; The Incoherence of the Incoherence*, trans. Simon van den Bergh (London: M. Luzac, 1954), 3; Barry S. Kogan, *Averroes and the Metaphysics of Causation* (Albany, NY: State University of New York Press, 1985), 27–45. Cf. Philo, *De opificio mundi*, IV-VI; Aquinas, *Summa Theologiæ*, II.1.2.
14 Francis Bacon, *Novum Organum*, ed. Joseph Devey (New York: P.F. Collier, 1902), 108–109.
15 Taylor, *Secular Age*, 37–38.
16 Dionysius the Areopagite, "The Divine Names," in *The Complete Works*, trans. Colm Luibheid (New York: Paulist Press, 1987), 708a.
17 Ibid., 593d, 708a.
18 René Descartes, *The Philosophical Writings of Descartes*, Vols. 1 and 2, trans. John Cottingham, Robert Stoothoff, and Dugald Murdoch (Cambridge: Cambridge University Press, 1984), 1:10, 13.
19 Nuno Fernandes, "Economic Effects of Coronavirus Outbreak (COVID-19) on the World Economy," (March 22, 2020). Available at SSRN: https://ssrn.com/abstract=3557504 or http://dx.doi.org/10.2139/ssrn.3557504; Andrew Atkeson, "What Will Be the Economic Impact of COVID-19 in the US? Rough Estimates of Disease Scenarios," *The National Bureau of Economic Research*, no. 26867 (March 2020). Available at: https://www.nber.org/papers/w26867.
20 Rabah Arezki, Daniel Lederman, Amani Abou Harb, Nelly El-Mallakh, Rachel Yuting Fan, Asif Islam, Ha Nguyen, and Marwane Zouaidi, "How Transparency Can Help the Middle East and North Africa," in *Middle East and North Africa Economic Update* (Washington, DC: World Bank, 2020), 6–14, 20–39; David Banks, Laura Albert, Jonathan Caulkins, Sylvia Fruhwirth-Schnatter, Fiona Greig, Adrian Raftery, and Duncan Thomas, "A Conversation about COVID-19 with Economists, Sociologists, Statisticians, and Operations Researchers," *Harvard Data Science Review* (May 22, 2020), Available at: https://doi.org/10.1162/99608f92.7fa08812.
21 Vikram Thakur and Anu Jain, "COVID 2019-Suicides: A Global Psychological Pandemic," *Brain, Behavior, and Immunity* S0889-1591(20)30643-7 (April 23, 2020). Available at: doi:10.1016/j.bbi.2020.04.062; Danijela Godinic, Obrenovic Bojan, and Khudaykulov Akmal, "Effects of Economic Uncertainty on Mental Health in the COVID-19 Pandemic Context: Social Identity Disturbance, Job Uncertainty and Psychological Well-Being Model," *International Journal of Innovation and Economic Development* 6,

no. 1 (2019), 61–74; Steven Taylor, *The Psychology of Pandemics: Preparing for the Next Global Outbreak of Infectious Disease* (Cambridge: Cambridge Scholars Publishing, 2019), 23–38.
22 Paul Collier, "Capitalism after Coronavirus," *NewStatesman*, May 6, 2020, Available at: https://www.newstatesman.com/politics/economy/2020/05/capitalism-after-coronavirus.
23 Sotiris Vardoulakis, Guy Marks, and Michael J. Abramson, "Lessons Learned from the Australian Bushfires: Climate Change, Air Pollution, and Public Health," *JAMA Internal Medicine* 180, no. 5 (2020), 635–636; Aiguo Dai, "Increasing Drought under Global Warming in Observations and Models," *Nature Climate Change* 3 (2013), 52–58.
24 Yuner Zhu, King-Wa Fu, Karen A. Grépin, Hai Liang, and Isaac Chun-Hai Fung, "Limited Early Warnings and Public Attention to Coronavirus Disease 2019 in China, January–February, 2020: A Longitudinal Cohort of Randomly Sampled Weibo Users," *Disaster Medicine and Public Health Preparedness* (2020), 1–4, https://doi.org/10.1017/dmp.2020.68; Rahul Chaturvedi and Rodney A. Gabriel, "COVID-19 Healthcare Delivery Impact on African Americans," *Disaster Medicine and Public Health Preparedness* (2020), 1–3, https://doi.org/10.1017/dmp.2020.179.
25 Luis P. Villarreal and Guenther Witzany, "Viruses Are Essential Agents within the Roots and Stem of the Tree of Life," *Journal of Theoretical Biology* 262, no. 4 (February 21, 2010), 698–710; Bertsy Goic and Maria-Carla Saleh, "Living with the Enemy: Viral Persistent Infections from a Friendly Viewpoint," *Current Opinion in Microbiology* 15, no. 4 (August 1, 2012), 531–37; Patrick Forterre, "Defining Life: The Virus Viewpoint," *Origins of Life and Evolution of Biospheres* 40, no. 2 (March 14, 2010), 151–160.
26 Luis P. Villarreal and Guenther Witzany, "When Competing Viruses Unify: Evolution, Conservation, and Plasticity of Genetic Identities," *Journal of Molecular Evolution* 80, no. 5–6 (June 19, 2015), 315.
27 César Asensio, Pierre Aumond, Arnaud Can, Luis Gascó, Peter Lercher, Jean-Marc Wunderli, Catherine Lavandier et al. "A Taxonomy Proposal for the Assessment of the Changes in Soundscape Resulting from the COVID-19 Lockdown," *International Journal of Environmental Research and Public Health* 17, no. 12 (2020), 4206.
28 Amanda Hess, "The Rise of the Coronavirus Nature Genre," *New York Times*, April 17, 2020, Available at: https://www.nytimes.com/2020/04/17/arts/coronavirus-nature-genre.html.
29 *Phaedo*, 99c ff.
30 See Alexander J.B. Hampton, "Christian Platonism, Nature and Environmental Crisis," in *Christian Platonism: A History*, eds. Alexander J.B. Hampton and John P. Kenney (Cambridge: Cambridge University Press, 2020), forthcoming.
31 Aquinas, *Summa Theologiæ*, 1a.2.1.
32 See Alexander J.B. Hampton, "The Poetics of Nature," in *Cambridge Companion to Religion and the Environment*, eds. Alexander J. B. Hampton and Douglas Hedley (Cambridge: Cambridge University Press), forthcoming.
33 William Wordsworth, *Tintern Abbey*, l. 96.
34 I Cor 12:12; *Phaedrus* 429d.
35 See Alexander J.B. Hampton, "A Post-Secular Nature and the New Nature Writing," *Christianity and Literature* 67 (2018), 454–471.

3 What happened to touch?

Richard Kearney

In this chapter I propose to address the crisis of touch during the coronavirus pandemic in relation to two contemporary concerns—digital communication and ecological connection.

Touch and digital communication

Touch is never so obvious as when confronted with its opposite—the untouchable. The imperative of social distancing, mandated in early 2020 because of the coronavirus, COVID-19, made us acutely aware of how central touch is to our lives. The threat of contagion through physical contact meant tactile encounters were kept to a minimum if not outlawed—everyone a potential carrier of the invisible virus. We could no longer reach out to touch others or touch our own faces with our hands (rapidly realizing just how often we do it). In my personal case, I was unable to hug my daughter in quarantine, or to travel to visit a dying relative. I was also not able to teach my students face to face—as classes went online—or shake hands with good colleagues and friends. When I turned a doorknob I became aware—as never before—how many others had turned that knob before me. As COVID-19 necessitated separation and isolation, everyone became aware of how much tangible space we share with each other every day; and how often we say 'let's keep in touch' when we are about to do the very opposite—say goodbye.

The more touch is forbidden, the more one desires it and appreciates how vital it is to our lives. Much in the same way that death—where the tactile body ceases—reminds us how tangible our existence is. It is when the hammer breaks that you appreciate the hammer. When the engine fails that you notice the engine. When someone dies that you miss them, newly conscious of what that person meant to you. So just as death makes us prize life, when touch is taken from us we realize how much it matters.

As I went into isolation in the days following lockdown in Spring 2020 I found myself visited by multiple memories of touch. The hot breath of my mother blowing against my five-year-old shoulders warming me up after a swim in the Irish Sea. The cool palm of my grandmother on my brow as I suffered fever. The brush of my first girlfriend's lips as we danced a slow dance. The smooth skin of my newly born child. Feelings welled up from involuntary memory—keeping me in touch with myself and the world. And other people told me of similar experiences: unexpected messages from old friends and old flames (the 'ex-factor') wishing to reconnect at a time when physical travel and tactile contact was suddenly suspended; a rush on online movies about romance, animals and nature; a raw yearning to eat one's favorite foods now that restaurants were closed, trips to food stores limited and culinary savors at a premium. The rarer tactile experience became, the more it was valued.

But touch was not the only sense affected by COVID-19. As widely reported, loss of taste and smell were symptoms of early infection. This struck me as curious given that these same senses were greatly diminished when homo sapiens became homo erectus, rising up from his four-legged posture on earth.[1] Losing our quadruped existence with animals, we raised our heads toward the sky, becoming 'upward gazers' (*anthropoi*). Henceforth, the eye became the dominant sense 'surveying all that man possessed' and suspending our close cohabitation with non-human beings. The first step toward the Anthropocene was taken as we lost touch with our primal embodiment. Hands no longer touched the earth but reached toward the stars. And we never again felt quite at ease in our skin. Clothes—made from hides of slaughtered animals—replaced hair as the means to protect our nakedness. As in the biblical Fall from nature, our 'first parents' covered their flesh with the skin of the snake that seduced them.

COVID-19 signaled the compromise of our 'animal' senses—touch, taste and smell—compelling us to live through the eye more than at any time in history. With the outbreak of the pandemic, the world went online. Though protective barriers were established against touching, tasting or inhaling the virus, our eyes worked overtime scouring our screens for news of the sickness: global broadcasts flashing from monitors illustrated by the macroscopic image of the microscopic 'enemy'—a little globe with sprouting red flowers (corona-tions?): the invisible virus made visible. And the online migration spread right across the board. Work—for those who still had it—largely became a matter of virtual communication from home. As did most of our social relations. Friendship parties, support rallies, music choirs,

What happened to touch? 31

reading groups, yoga labs, together-apart theatre projects, spiritual meetings, internet masses, fitness clubs and family reunions all rapidly multiplied on the web. Even Zoom weddings and funerals became common occurrences, while distance education was de rigueur with classes conducted exclusively online. Internet shopping and home delivery saved us going to the shops; and tele-doctoring removed the need to travel to clinics and hospitals, unless absolutely necessary. During the lockdown no one moved without 'essential' cause. In the first quarter of 2020, the virus went viral. Homo sapiens became homo cybernens—our sojourn on the web sedulously preparing us for life in a post-pandemic world.

But what we lost on the roundabout we may have won on the swings. Once COVID-19 arrived—traveling stealthily east to west—humanity needed all its wits about it. If the state of exception was a state of excarnation it was also a call to 'connect' by other means. Videos of sorrow and joy mushroomed on the internet. Heartrending tales of dying loved ones trended alongside clips of ingenious hilarity. Facetime farewells and terminal appeals to Alexa[2] were followed by mischievous memes of irreverent wit. (A favorite was Winnie the Pooh turning to a clingy Piglet shouting 'Back the f... up'.) And in addition to these upswells of popular imagination, the web summoned some of its most artful professionals to its side. Within no time, top media outlets were commissioning reflections from the most gifted writers of our time—scientists, doctors, artists and poets—posting them online for millions to read; and it was surprising how many of them spoke about *touch*. The *New York Review* featured a series of remarkable reflections under the title, 'Pandemic Journal',[3] while *Le Monde* published a weekly column of deeply moving testimonies, including a homage to the power of skin by novelist Leïla Slamani:

> Naked skin of the new born placed on its mother's breast. Skin exposed to the sun's caress before the gaze of a lover. Skin shivering at the brush of a hand. Children know the palliative power of touch. Since at night, frightened of monsters and darkness, they take our hands and place them on their bare skin, their trembling bodies.[4]

These epidermal scenes, triggered by the prohibition against touch, reminded Slamani of just how endangered tactility is in our age (where, she writes, the thing we touch most is our smartphone); she ends with a plea for touch as our most vital sense. Meanwhile, in *Corriere della Serra*, Julia Kristeva observed how the pandemic was compelling us to confront our basic fragility, exposing three core problems of 'globalized man' in the digital age: solitude experienced as loneliness, intolerance of limits and the repression of our mortality. She wrote:

> I am struck by our contemporary incapacity to be alone. All this hyper-connected exaltation makes us live in isolation in front of screens. This has not abolished loneliness, but has ensconced it in the social media, has compressed it in messages and data. People already devastated by loneliness find themselves alone today, because although they have words, signs, icons, they have lost the flesh of words, sensations, sharing, tenderness, duty towards the other, care for the other. We give the flesh of words as a sacrificial offering to the virus and to malady, but we were already orphans of that human dimension that is shared passion. All of a sudden we realize that we are alone and that we have lost touch with our inner core. We are slaves of the screens that have not at all abolished loneliness but have only absorbed it. This is where the recent anxiety and anger are coming from.[5]

On the more positive side, Kristeva surmised that the viral crisis had triggered a 'revelation of life as a whole, starting with everyone's vulnerability with regard to pleasure and sexuality', and that it is preparing us 'for a new art of living that will be complex and daring'.[6]

This 'new art' will comprise, among other things, novel initiatives with regard to touch. If COVID-19 reinforced a regime of excarnation— in hitherto unforeseen ways—it also witnessed a proliferation of digital experiments with the senses. In a curious irony, as we forfeited the option of direct touch, ingenious alternatives were sought through technology. Under the banner, *'social distancing doesn't have to mean disconnecting'*, innovative projects flourished using Virtual Reality and Augmented Reality tele-haptics. One noteworthy example was the Altspace program of meet-ups between families and friends separated by the pandemic censure of physical proximity.[7] Using VR headsets and simple web browsers lowering barriers of entry, the project fostered multiple kinds of inventive gatherings—social interactions, haptic journeys, tele-therapies, spiritual liturgies, synesthetic presentations. Such multi-sensory gatherings enabled spatially separated participants to meet in a common space (a synesthetic version of chat room interactions of the 1990s).[8] Loved ones greeted each other with tele-haptic hugs across impossible differences of location and time.[9] Even experiments with synthetic skin were devised to allow a tactile sense of 'felt' empathy with 'distanced' friends.[10] This intensified use of social VR via Altspace and other tele-haptic projects served as a laboratory for new possibilities of connecting across distance, bringing the far near and making the strange more familiar. In particular, the opening up of alternative public health therapies via technology added a whole new dimension to tele-medicine, representing yet another creative response to COVID-19.

What is striking about these tele-haptic experiments is that their inventors, faced with the eclipse of touch, devised new means to combine the powers of virtual and tactile bodies. They made scarcity the mother of invention, exploring hybrid modes of haptic communication that challenged old mind-body dualisms and defied the dichotomy between technology and life. They testified to the desperate human need to touch and be touched, come what may. The ineradicable desire for tangible contact. It remains to be seen, of course, whether such leaps into unchartered territories of tactility succeed in becoming part of our post-pandemic future. Or do so in a life-enhancing way. The important thing, however, is that when faced with the loss of carnal contact the human imagination responded by contriving new possibilities of haptic communion. When one kind of touch was in trouble, another came to the rescue.

One of the most important lessons of COVID-19 is, I believe, the question of 'connection'. From the earliest of times touch was seen as a power of healing through accompaniment. It was deemed an indispensable gift to the commons of the body. A medium of savvy and tact, of flair and vision. In the oldest stories of the wisdom traditions—from Jacob and Jesus to Chiron and Asclepius—the double sensibility of healer and healed entailed the double sensation of touching and being touched. Few lessons are more urgent for us today when digital communication and tactile contact are called to convene for the future health of humanity. If we only keep in touch. If we only connect.

So my question is this: can digital culture, critically deployed, address the question of 'touch' for new generations? Can certain forms of digital pedagogy serve as creative alternatives and antidotes to our simulation crisis by engaging directly with our contemporary media of communication? Like the 'hair of the dog', might a good response to digital abuse be digital re-use? Namely digital technology putting itself in question and re-opening spaces where we might invent new ways to re-inhabit our world—what I call 'ana-technology' (from the Greek *ana*, meaning up, again, anew in time and space).

These concerns inform the thinking of several recent digital literacy campaigns and groups like Digital Action for Democracy—which invigilate our cyber culture and keep it honest —as well as pioneering efforts to devise new compacts between the virtual and the real. I am thinking especially of cutting-edge projects with digital storytelling and VR technology at the MIT Open Doc Lab and Public VR Lab in Boston. The latter, for instance, hosts a participatory storytelling project, 'Arrival VR', where participants are invited to enter virtual worlds where they empathize with immigrants and interact in common collaborative spaces—galleries, classrooms, town halls, museums, art labs and community centers—exploring encounters with others in their life-world. Such projects in 'empathy' are partly inspired by recent experiments in the amplification of touch by digital technology—notably the 2019 tree experiment with haptic vests enabling participants to 'feel' what it is like to be a tree growing and expanding; or the use of haptic prostheses to 'feel' the embrace of fellow humans removed in space or time. These ventures in hapto-technology are still embryonic, to be sure, but I believe they portend productive possibilities of collusion between virtual and embodied experience—ways in which our real and simulated worlds may cooperate rather than compete, avoiding rigid dualisms of artificial and tactile intelligence. For there is surely no point replacing the Platonic dichotomy of mind versus body with a 'postmodern' equivalent. The challenge is to find new modalities of accommodation between our digital and lived bodies, acknowledging their differences while exploring modes of mutually enhancing symbiosis. This is arguably one of the most vital tasks for our emerging Symbiocene, the connectedness between all sentient beings, which responds to the demands of the 'reciprocity principle' for our time. As we move from the Anthropocene of optocentric dominance to a Symbiocene of collaboration between tactile and digital therapies, the question of healing the whole person—and planet—is crucial.

But, in the wake of COVID-19, we must begin again with little things. Modest gestures. In addition to systemic leaps, addressing our global pandemic crisis, we need to take small steps, one at a time. Here are some simple examples of what symbiotic gestures of collaboration might include in post-pandemic everyday life. Using GPS to navigate our journeys while not hesitating to ask people in the street for directions or to wander down unchartered paths and be surprised by what we find. Plugging into iTunes with headphones but also finding time to listen to random sounds of winds, birds, sirens and silence. Asking Siri and Alexa to do our bidding without ceasing to use our bodies in the service of others—placing a hand on a shoulder to show care. Watching movies on computer screens while also visiting movie houses, theaters and live shows where a sense of shared community can trigger unexpected feelings of solidarity and compassion. Ordering books online, googling databases and taking remote education courses (mandatory during lockdown and social isolation), without forgetting to browse volumes in bookstores and libraries or attend 'live' classes in the presence of living teachers (where possible and permissible). Enjoying e-sports, e-entertainment and e-travel without forgoing the excitement of huddling in stadiums with living bodies or traveling physically to places where we encounter real strangers in strange worlds. Using online banking and shopping but also trading once again with actual people in markets and malls, when restrictions are lifted. Profiting fully from tele-doctoring, AI readings of X-Rays and novel forms of imaging technology without forfeiting moments of physical contact between healer and healed. And, finally, connecting daily with others online while also finding time to converse with tangibly present persons face to face. In short, let's make the most of digital technology but never forget the real thing.

Ultimately, it is a matter of both/and. It is clear that to live fully in a post-pandemic world we will need both virtual imagination *and* incarnate action. Both digital touch and live touch. The connectivity of the World Wide Web and the commons of the body. No one can deny the extraordinary advantages of digital technology—nowhere more evident than during the socially distant lockdowns of 2020. The gains are too great to ignore in the name of some nostalgia for bygone times. In the end it is a matter of striking the right balance between the virtual and the tactile, not choosing one over the other. To recover our senses today is to remain sensitive to both carnal and cyber existence. To honor the vital human need for 'double sensibility'. Imagining and living in concert. Touching and being touched in good measure.

Touch and ecological connection

After COVID-19 what healing touch is possible? During the pandemic curtailment of touch in medical treatment, I was acutely reminded not only of the therapeutic importance of our tactile body but also of our relationship to the animal and natural world.[11] At the time I was completing a book entitled *Touch: Recovering our Most Vital Sense*, in which I suggested that any attempt to create a salutary 'commons of the body' must include the animal world—the place we all began. Especially when it comes to tactile healing.

Somatic therapy, focused on the mammalian limbic brain, has been known to benefit from work with animals such as horses, dogs and dolphins. Equine-assisted therapy uses horses as transferential objects for PTSD and autistic patients, enabling them to recover tactile communication by relating affectively with non-human beings. Since horses are mostly tangible skin with minimal fur, scales or carapace covering the body, they respond readily to the slightest touch. Their hide keeps the score. Alert and attentive, they are carnally attuned, all flesh so to speak. The therapeutic role of dogs and other 'care animals' in the work of attunement is also well known. The healing power of dogs goes back to the beginning of human history. Forty thousand-year-old cave fossils show human and canine footprints side by side; and ancient and medieval legends abound in tales of healers with dogs. Chiron the wounded healer was accompanied by his dog in Greek mythology and his disciple, Asclepius, was said to appear in the dream form of a dog with patients feeling a canine tongue salving their scars. And one might also cite the popular medieval depictions of St. Roch (Rocco) being saved by a dog licking his wounds. St. Roch became the patron saint of canines and was often invoked as talismanic protection against sickness and plague. Recent research in animal behavior science reveals that the bonding hormone, oxytocin, is released in both dogs and humans when they come into caring contact (similar to the bonding between mother and child). A 2015 study in the journal *Behavioral Processes* indicates that dogs respond therapeutically by means of special scent and sound. So-called 'care dogs' have become common in contemporary health culture where tactile contact plays a crucial role; and in his breakthrough book on trauma and healing, *The Body Keeps the Score*, Bessel Van der Kolk quotes research of dogs and horses being successfully used to treat groups of trauma patients. He cites the example of a young woman who was healed from deep suicidal depression by equine therapy with a horse she worked with: 'She started to feel a visceral connection with another creature and began to talk to him like a friend. Gradually she started talking with the other kids in the program and eventually, with her counselor'.[12]

Less well known perhaps is the practice of Kangaroo Mother Care (KMC)—another example of human health care learning from animals. This work, pioneered by the French Columbian pediatrician, Nathalie Charpak, focuses on the care of low-birth rate preterm infants being held close to the chest and tummy of the mother (as in the pouch). This provides the natural-animal-human equivalent to hospital incubation in developed medical cultures, permitting premature babies not only to survive but to flourish even better than in clinical incubators with drips and feeds. The evidence shows that infant flourishing is as much about attachment as alimentation. During the coronavirus pandemic, the question of parents touching newly born infants and children touching terminally ill parents (especially in nursing care homes) became a deeply emotional and often tragic phenomenon.

In his book, *Our Wild Calling: How Connecting with Animals Can Transform Our Lives—and Save Theirs*, nature scholar, Richard Louv, rehearses persuasive stories of how humans and animals heal each other through mutual attunement. 'In the habitat of the heart', he writes,

> in that whisper of recognition between two beings when time seems to stop, when space assumes a different shape—in that moment, we sense a shared soul. That is what connects the woman and the bear, the diver and the octopus, the dog and the child, the boy and the jaguar, the fisherman and the golden eagles on the shore.[13]

Louv makes a plea for a therapeutic reconnection with the tangible world of nature—noting what he calls our growing Nature Deficit Disorder. The dramatic decline of thousands of animal and plant species is telling: between 1970 and 2014 the global wildlife population shrank by 60% according to World Wildlife Fund statistics. Louv cites various eco-psychological studies about how animal-assisted therapies—and intimate proximity to trees and plants—can reduce symptoms of illness and realign our sense of well-being. Such ecological therapies, he argues, are intimately related to our inclusiveness in the natural world; for while digital gaming technology (for example, the 2016 online game *No Man's Sky*) can generate countless new 'virtual species' through leaps of fantasy, the full reparation of our life-world requires that we get back in touch with our animal-terrestrial being. We need both. Louv concludes that reversing the biodiversity collapse and climate threat cannot be accomplished solely through technology or institutional politics, but requires a more affective connection to the family of animals and plants, acknowledging the 'inescapable network of mutuality' that Martin Luther King called for among beings.[14]

To this end, Louv advocates an advance toward a new 'Symbiocene': an age of therapeutic connectedness going beyond the Anthropocene of contemporary excarnation and 'encompassing reciprocity and redistribution, where wildness survives, albeit in newer forms and in unexpected places, where we live in balance with other life'.[15] This includes a strong need to reconnect with nature and animals and I think it is no accident that one of most pioneering early research projects in haptic VR was the 'Tree Experiment' where, as mentioned, humans wore haptic vests to 'feel' the experience of a tree moving in the wind.

The tree carries a basic archetypal power for humans from the beginning of time, manifest in all great wisdom traditions. (If you have any doubts read Richard Powers' *The Overstory*).

Referring to COVID-19, Richard Rohr notes that the desire for tactile connection represents a fundamental need to go beyond oneself to 'otherness'; and he cites African American mystic, Howard Thurman, who understood this as a complicity with nature which provided him with 'a certain overriding immunity against the pains in life'.[16] In his youth Thurman found solace in a relationship with a tree near his home: Eventually he discovered that the oak tree and he had a unique relationship. 'I could sit, *my back against its trunk*...and reach down into the quiet places of my spirit, take out my bruises and joys, unfold them and talk about them. I could talk aloud to the oak tree and know that I was understood. It too, was part of my reality, like the woods ... giving me space'.[17] The culture of social distancing from other humans is perhaps an opportunity for us to practice 'ecotherapy' (in Japanese Zen philosophy, *Shinrin-yoku*)—namely, healing by contact with trees and forests. A possibility for a newfound appreciation for the outdoors when this time of 'sheltering in' is over.[18]

Such connectedness demands the extension of a 'double sensibility principle' beyond human to other-than-human creatures. It calls for a hands-on 'Reciprocity Principle' between all creatures, following simple steps:

> For every moment of healing that humans receive from another creature, humans will provide an equal moment of healing for that animal and its kin. For every dollar we spend on classroom technology, we will spend at least another dollar creating chances for children to connect deeply with another animal, plant or person. For every day of loneliness we endure, we'll spend a day in communion with the life around us until the loneliness passes away.[19]

And we might add, for every moment we connect digitally in our postpandemic world we will connect carnally, where safety and sensitivity permit.

A final word on the theological implications of post-pandemic touch. While most religious services and liturgies went online during the lockdown, there was a pervasive need for physical contact—laying on of hands, eucharist on tongues, chalices on tables—in hospitals and nursing homes when it came to chaplains delivering last rites and final prayers with patients dying of the virus.[20] This was true for all spiritual confessions, and for Christians it served as a reminder of the primary message of Christ's incarnation: Christ became flesh in order to heal the sick with his hands. A message dramatically portrayed in the paradigmatic Gospel scene of the bleeding woman who touches the hem of Jesus's cloak and is healed. A typical example of the reciprocity principle of touch.[21]

Notes

1. *See* John Manoussakis, "Coronations: Notes from the Quarantine," *The New Polis*, April 10, 2020.

   Keeping in mind the distinction between senses of distance and senses of proximity, I find it quite suggestive that the symptoms through which COVID-19 manifests itself—apart from those that it shares in common with the rest of respiratory infections, such a coughing and fever—are precisely anosmia and ageusia, that is, the inability of the infected person to smell and to taste. Without such tactile senses that operate by de-distancing, to borrow Heidegger's expression, the virus compromises one's health by depriving him of his sense of proximity. It has been speculated that the characteristic upright posture of a human being as well as its coordinating bipedalism became the evolutionary results of a human's need to rely more on his sight and less on his smell. By standing up, smell—the predominant sense for social interaction among animals—was replaced for man by sight.

2. *See* the tragic case of Lou Ann Dagen, a 66-year-old resident of a Michigan nursing home, who begged Alexa 40 times for help before dying alone (April 7, 2020), as her solitary recordings revealed.
3. *New York Review*, Vol LXVII, no 7, April 2020.
4. Leïla Slamani, "*L'Epidémie de Coronavirus vient nous accentuer une tendance: Nous touchons de moins en moins la peau de l'autre,*" *Le Monde*, April 2020, transl. Richard Kearney.
5. Julia Kristeva, "Humanity Is Rediscovering Existential Solitude, the Meaning of Limits and Mortality," interview by Stefano Montefiori, transl. Mariya Chokova, *Corriere della Serra*, March 29, 2020.
6. Ibid.
7. Regarding haptic applications of social VR on Altspace, *see* https://www.vrfitnessinsider.com/haptics-thrilling-prospect. It is telling how in the case of internet masses, seders and prayer meetings during the lockdown, participants felt a strong desire to hold tactile cups, chalices, candles or bread in their hands as they participated 'remotely' in the virtual ceremonies.
8. *See* https://educatorsinvr.com/events/international-summit/. For different social VR examples: https://lab.onebonsai.com/social-vr-is-the-weird-future-of-social-media-2fedf4663011.
9. *See* https://www.ign.com/articles/mother-plays-with-deceased-daughter-in-vr-recreation and https://www.vrfitnessinsider.com/haptics-thrilling-prospect/.
10. *See* https://singularityhub.com/2019/11/25/synthetic-skin-is-bringing-a-sense-of-touch-to-virtual-reality/. For a timely discussion of empathy and the VR relationship between digital storytelling, tele-haptics and viscerality, *see*

https://teslasuit.io/blog/empathy-virtual-reality/. And for more of the science behind it: https://www.sciencedaily.com/releases/2019/11/191120131255.htm. I am grateful to Kathy Bisbee, director of the Brookline Interactive Project for this information.

11 Richard Kearney, *Touch: Recovering Our Most Vital Sense* (New York: Columbia University Press, 2020).
12 Bessel Van der Kolk, *The Body Keeps the Score: Brain, Mind, and Body in the Healing of Trauma* (New York: Penguin Books, 2014), 82, 153.
13 Richard Louv, *Our Wild Calling: How Connecting with Animals Can Transform Our Lives—and Save Theirs* (Chapel Hill: Algonquin Books, 2019), 272.
14 Martin Luther King Jr., *Letter from Birmingham Jail: Martin Luther King Jr.'s Letter from Birmingham Jail and the Struggle That Changed a Nation* (April 16, 1963).
15 Louv, *Our Wild Calling*, 273.
16 Howard Thurman, *With Head and Heart: The Autobiography of Howard Thurman* (Orlando: Harcourt Brace, 1979), 8.
17 Thurman, *With Head and Heart*, 8.
18 See Rohr, *Action and Contemplation Reflection*, April 18, 2020. See Peter Wohlleben, *The Hidden Life of Trees: What They Feel, How They Communicate, Discoveries from a Secret World*, transl. Jane Billinghurst (Vancouver: Greystone Books, 2015), Available at: https://cac.org/the-universal-pattern-weekly-summary-2020-04-18/.
19 Louv, *Our Wild Calling*, 273. Louv relates his reciprocity principle to Martin Buber's I/Thou.
20 Elizabeth Dias, "The Last Anointing," *New York Times*, June 6, 2020.
21 "She had heard about Jesus and came up behind him in the crowd and touched his cloak. She said: 'if I but touch (*hapsomai*) his clothes, I shall be cured'. Immediately her flow of blood dried up. She felt in her body that she was healed of her affliction. Jesus, aware at once that power had gone out from him, turned around in the crowd and asked: 'Who has touched me?'" Mark 5:27–31. For a detailed analysis *see* Kearney, *Touch*, Chapter 3, "Wounded Healers".

4 The gallop of the pale green horse

Pandemic, pandemonium and panentheism

Catherine Keller

Amidst the early Spring greening of my city, one could barely hear the hoofbeats over the roar of traffic. But they came closer, louder, until a voice shouted "'Come!' I looked and there was a pale green horse."[1] And it came galloping in, death-ridden, spreading "pestilence." The traffic din faded, the city shut down, scholars got some extra time for their writing. Mine turned eerie, as I was just about done with *Apocalypse After All?*, and therefore mentally prepared for new historic levels of crisis.[2] The hallucinogenic metaphors—metaforces—of John of Patmos depict "coming" political, economic and ecological catastrophe. They offer of course no predictions of events twenty centuries in their future, but rather—read in their over-reaching relevance—a prophetic encryption of deep civilizational patterns already locked in by the Roman Empire. I had however written nothing on the threat of a pandemic; I had ignored the fourth horseman. As for most of the academic left, pandemic was one issue I never included in my lists of sex, race, class, climate, etc.

I will however refrain from declaring the coronapocalypse. I hope that even as you read this, COVID-19 is galloping off into the sunset of fading relevance. If it is, or if it is not, I hope also that the pandemic's revelation is *not* dissipating into mere normality. *Apokalypsis* retains its original meaning as unveiling, dis/closure. Not final closure. You will recall that it is the Lamb—the mute and bloody quadruped Christ— who opens the seven seals. With each of the first four seals, one of the "four creatures" thunders out: "Come!" And a horse comes forth.

The fourth creature, eagle-like, calls, and the pale green horse appears: "its rider's name was Death," able to kill with "famine, and pestilence, and by the wild animals of the earth." Unlike the others, this sickly green steed carries a set of nonhuman torments. Some sort of deadly payback—against a species turned destructive of the nonhuman? In a suggestive anachronism, our present pestilence probably has its origins in wild animals, bats or pangolins, not attacking us—but delivering the virus.

In the present meditation the rhythm of the ancient hoofbeats now fades into its anachronistic background. But you may hear it in the percussive alliteration of the pandemic with a certain pandæmonium and a possible panentheism.

Pandemic inhumanity

Once delivered, the virus morphed into its lethal form for interhuman transmission. Richard Ostfeld, a leading ecosystems scientist, writes in the *Scientific American* that "Rodents and some bats thrive when we disrupt natural habitats. They are the most likely to promote transmissions [of pathogens]. The more we disturb the forests and habitats the more danger we are in."[3] In other words, coronavirus should be read as an ecological, not merely medical, crisis. Vidal writes that

> Only a decade or two ago it was widely thought that tropical forests and intact natural environments teeming with exotic wildlife threatened humans by harboring the viruses and pathogens that lead to new diseases...like Ebola, HIV and dengue. But a number of researchers today think that it is actually humanity's destruction of biodiversity that creates the conditions for new viruses...like COVID-19...to arise—with profound health and economic impacts... In fact, a new discipline, planetary health, is emerging that focuses on the increasingly visible connections among the well-being of humans, other living things and entire ecosystems.[4]

The relation between the human and the nonhuman is irreducible to that between human and other animals. A more primal entanglement is in play: between what we consider life, the organic, and what is called nonlife, the chemical, the geological. It is of that indeterminate crossover, between organic and inorganic, that the coronavirus is so spitefully reminding us. Virologist Luis P. Villarreal warned early in this century that the ambiguous status of a virus—between biology and chemistry—was preventing adequate understanding—and therefore preparation for coming pandemics: "Regardless of whether or not we consider viruses to be alive, it is time to acknowledge and study them in their natural context—within the web of life."[5]

Of course the webbiness that has revealed itself with such poignancy during this time of our mutual untouchability has been primarily human. Endless articles on the (electronic) web have engaged the hope that we might, through this period of sheltering in place, come to a new collective awareness of our inseparability from each other, in any place. And these musings have not sounded like a clichéd "we're all connected," but like an actual ripple effect of fresh awareness. And because it is a global pandemic that so irrepressibly made the point, there is here also the chance of rethinking the interhuman as woven upon the inhuman. And that means that the virus, in its gray zone between life and nonlife, does its thing as part of the web of life.

That uncertain boundary between life and nonlife has haunted not just virology and related fields—but powerful reassessments of the human location within the web of life. The "human" itself breaks thereby into its entangled diversity—wild differences globally if never fully tamed and trapped by oppressions and exploitations twisted around relations that reach across the whole spectrum of life, a life that enfolds the apparently nonliving into its chaosmos.

In other words the virus—through no pedagogical intention of its own—offers a chance to strengthen the pandemically spreading sense of our creaturely connectivity. We may best take hold of that chance by linking that felt awareness into theories that have prepared the way of the insight. That way in this volume converges with certain theological pathways. So we may notice that the process theology sometimes nicknamed panentheism has always lived within a cosmology of radical interconnection: indeed "we find ourselves in a buzzing world, amid a democracy of fellow creatures."[6] That is of course the language of Alfred North Whitehead, whose vision was inspired not just to incorporate biological evolution but physics—the furthest from "life"—into a purposeful universe. Every creature, which is to "actual entity," is a momentary event of interrelation. Creatures differ endlessly from each other and from each others' species in levels and styles of complexity—but they all share a vibrancy, mostly unconscious, a pulse of experience, a feeling of relation: "Nature Alive."[7] Down to the quantum elements a responsive affectivity courses through—indeed co-creates—the world. Whitehead's primary influence has taken the form of over half a century of process theology. So what does this universe of entangled multiplicities mean theologically? Its panexperientialism of the very fiber of life is all woven into the integral experience of God. *Pan en theos.* We will return to that in the final section.

It might not be too late for a collective embrace of our radical interdependence. A theology of process will be an unavoidable resource. But a great shift of earthly thought needs a diverse and ever refreshed company of thinkers. They will be largely nontheists.

Hence Whitehead's influence upon Deleuze and so upon the current assemblages of so-called affect theorists as well as new materialists remains key (as explicitly in William Connolly, Brian Massumi, Jane Bennett, Bruno Latour). Other affinities remain indirect, and all the more important.

For instance, Kathryn Yusoff, scholar of "inhuman geography," writes the following: "The division of matter into nonlife and life pertains not only to matter but to the racial organization of life as foundational to New World geographies." In the radical revision of the field of geography "the inhuman is a call across categories, material and symbolic, corporeal and incorporeal, intimacies cut across life and nonlife…"[8] Interestingly at the end she says of her book, *A Billion Black Anthropocenes or None*, that it "goes in search of a grammar of geology for the storm next time."[9] Channeling James Baldwin, she was not predicting the pandemic. But she has revealed a depth geology of the civilization that colonized the nonhuman and the human planet for gain, with particular horror for those racial others who could not be counted as quite human, and so not even as quite fully alive. Black Lives. In perverse illustration, when I thought this chapter was done, the traumatic relevance of "Black Lives Matter" breaks across the news again. That mattering in Yusoff's analysis has geological repercussions.

So to embrace our intimacy with the inhuman is to answer to those dehumanized humans, even as we rediscover the nonhuman which we also are. But this conclusion bursts into the troubled world-present with particular force, not intended to be theological at all: she "asserts an insurgent geology for the end of the world, for the possibility of other worlds not marked by anti-Blackness, where the inhuman is a relation, no longer an appendage of fungibility."[10]

I appreciate her apocalypse—true *apokalypsis*, not prediction of final closure but dis/closure of possibility. In the meantime capital depends upon the fungible: the property of a commodity whose units are interchangeable, so that each of its parts is indistinguishable from the others. And commodified beings remain externally related to one another. The inhuman as a *relation*, by contrast, exemplifies Whitehead's notion of "internal relations." Each creature willy-nilly participates in the other creatures assembling its world, which itself partakes of each creature. If we have gotten cornered in a world—human and inhuman—made ever more fungible, the economics that colonizes the planet and that carried the virus may also be exposing its vulnerability: there flashes the chance of the end of its ever whitening and widening world. The possibility of other worlds…But that possibility does not open up without the disclosure of multiple entangled ills, globally crisscrossing, double crossing, and for a moment revealing themselves amid the planetary pandemic. To that multiplicity we now turn.

Pandemonium city

Pandemonium—was it mere alliteration linking it to pandemic in my head? The words seem disconnected, almost opposed: the pandemic has spread eerie silence and orderly separation more than any wild and noisy disorder. Then I remembered the original meaning of *pandemonium*—"all the demons." Got it. What a host of demons the pandemic has been revealing: not supernatural spooks but systems of normalized injustice—normally hidden in plain view. Like all smart demons.

For one: as the virus presented, so did the virulence of a national government repressive of science, of information, let alone of justice, and dismissive of its own responsibility to protect and care for its population. But the systemic, pre-pandemic torments are legion. As the United States election looms, so too the demons of democracy's doom. (I regret the necessity of lodging this entire meditation within a particular national perspective, and am grateful that this volume is not thus limited. Nor are the demons.) The protofascist power-demon locksteps with white supremacism: and it would portray the great late spring uprising of 2020 as the true pandemonium—to mask and justify its own pan-demonism. The trick of the systemic forces, taking metaphoric form in this reflection as demons, is, of course, *their* demonization of requisite alien and enemy others.

As to that specific supremacist demon vis-à-vis the virus: the stunning statistics of the disproportionate racial impact reveal nothing new about us/US. But they do reveal. Consider how "African Americans represent a third of all deaths from COVID-19, even though they represent only 13% of the national population."[11] This disparity brings home the flagrant inhumanity of racism built into the housing, jobs, education, pollution, asthma, healthcare, of racially segregated cities. Such disparity requires policing. And amidst the breath-taking inequalities exposed by the pandemic, the name of George Floyd suddenly breaks across the diseased US like another seal opening.

If neoliberal capitalism relies upon the exploitation—and its shadowing demonization—of black and brown people, this does not mean that race can be identified with poverty. People of color rise to great financial success, and conversely, racism impacts middle-class and wealthy blacks but not middle-class and wealthy whites. And global economics has its own hyperdrive. It is rather that racism prances arm in arm with capitalism. In the lead-up to the uprising, the economics of pandemonium had layoffs and unemployment rates exceeded only by the Great Depression. Close by a demon of food insecurity prances across the US, and look, there is the spirit of ageism. And the religious right grabs the chance to trot out its added demons, finding in the pandemic "God's consequential wrath" against those with a "proclivity toward lesbianism and homosexuality....and who practice 'the religion of environmentalism.'"[12]

And what of the earth-sized demon of ecological destruction and its choir of deniers? No one blames the pandemic on climate change or carbon emissions. But neither can it be explained apart from the relentless human destruction of nonhuman habitats. Nor can it be separated from the global capitalism and travel that both carry the virus and warm the planet.

The fever of the earth and the fever of COVID-19 have different causes—but they present as symptoms of the same planetary pandemonium. For all its epochal heat, global warming has remained on the back burner of most people's consciousness. It appears to move slowly—we think we'll die of old age before it gets dire. In the meantime, denial reigns. Never mind that, say, a dam in Michigan just collapsed due to catastrophic flooding—forcing not only thousands to flee but also stirring worry over possible toxic pollution.[13] The unprecedented floods and storms, heat and droughts are treated—no matter what the science says—as exceptions. The double denialism of Trump's treatment of COVID-19 and of environmental regulation: a match made in hell. I mean that literally. Indeed quite literarily.[14]

The word "pandemonium," it turns out, was invented by John Milton—*Pandæmonium* is the capital of Hell in his epic poem, Paradise Lost—"the high Capital Of Satan and his Peers."[15] All those demons. But it is not Satan himself who envisioned this elegant new city. It is none other than *Mammon*, the biblical demon of economic avarice, who directs its construction. Mammon organizes demons and humans to mine the Earth for its "treasures"—by which he builds the golden splendor of *Pandæmonium*:

> Men also, and by [Mammon's] suggestion taught,
> Ransack'd the Center, and with impious hands
> Rifl'd the bowels of thir mother Earth
> For Treasures better hid. Soon had his crew
> Op'nd into the Hill a spacious wound
> And dig'd out ribs of Gold.[16]

In view of this violent plunder of the planet, Milton goes on to warn, "let none admire/ That riches grow in Hell...."[17]

By a noteworthy synchronicity, Milton was not writing *Paradise Lost* at home in the capital city of London, which he had fled with his family in 1664 to escape the last outbreak of bubonic plague. On the wake of increased global travel and trade, thought to have come from a region in China by way of the Silk Road or the new schooner ships, that plague remains the second worst pandemic in history, at least for now. It killed a quarter of the city's population in 18 months: an estimated 100,000.

The epic hell revealed by our present pandemonium can again be masked as normality and order: not as the therapeutic order of social distancing and measured re-openings, but as the old order that formed civilization, *civis*, city (I will only mention that the dragon, two beasts and great whore form the head demons of Revelation's empire). The ancient and hypermodern order ever mutating imposes as normal its earth-wounding systems of greed and power. Business as usual.

None of these systemic demons are new. But they have taken ever new forms of exploitation, enslavement, extraction. And at this moment, these pan-demons dance garishly into view through the pandemic interruption of normalcy—and so they too get denormalized for a moment. And they seem just too much. Too many. Too many feverish issues to address all at once. Too many for the righteous "I told you so's" of any single-issue movement. Too many to hold in view together. Between exhausting us with their too-muchness and seducing us with their "back to normal," the orderly disorder of our *Pandæmonium* may prevail for a tragically foreseeable future.

Or on the other hand, the pandemic interruption may help us to face, to think, to confront the interconnectivity of all of our many, too many, burning issues. The Black womanist trope of "intersectionalism" captures the realization that questions of race come bound with those of sexuality and class. And even geology. If the coronapocalypse has so rudely reminded us of the intimate intersection between life and nonlife, it unveils (apokalypsis) the pan-demonic dance and disfiguration of our material relatedness. Our mattering intersections.

Are we now beginning to move in a dance of death disguised as a return to normal? Back through the city gates of Pandemonium?

Pan en theos

Might we together move against the pressure of mere return? In an essay that went, yes, viral, the Indian novelist Arundhati Roy put this choice gorgeously:

> Nothing could be worse than a return to normality. Historically, pandemics have forced humans to break with the past and imagine

their world anew. This one is no different. It is a portal, a gateway between one world and the next. We can choose to walk through it, dragging the carcasses of our prejudice and hatred, our avarice, our data banks and dead ideas, our dead rivers and smoky skies behind us. Or we can walk through lightly, with little luggage, ready to imagine another world. And ready to fight for it.[18]

Of course such secular imagining of a "next world," "another world" comes charged with theological associations. But Roy offers no fantasy of angels coming down to defeat demons; no escape through Peter's portal to heaven. Her pandemic portal offers no utopian, let alone supernatural guarantees. Nor does a responsible theology. We would not want to come burdened with dead gods and other old baggage. The fight for another world does, however, call upon something different from optimistic unreality or stoic courage. It calls us to embrace the *possibility* of such a world, to embrace it together, and so to find ourselves *gathering*—in touch if not touching—as we go.

For those of us who still (somehow) gather in religious assemblages, our traditions may strengthen that chance. Or they may sabotage it. Churches may simply slump back into their own fading normal; or worse, join the demons in demonizing the abnormal among them—queers, environmentalists and other heretics. And wait for omnipotent rescue. But some of our assemblages are biblically better-tuned; even the ancient prophetic figures of "the new heaven and earth" need translate no longer as supernatural intervention or afterlife escape. The new world—even John's New Jerusalem, mythic antitype of Milton's Pandemonium—evokes not a replacement of this earth, but its radical renewal.

In this work, panentheism names one cross-religious approach among many dedicated to the healing of our planetary entanglement. It is just one way—contested among process theologians—of naming the work of process theology. I appeal to it long before pandemic pandemonium because it manages to name so much in a word. *All in God*, that is, the pan of the entangled immensity that is not just a world but all possible worlds, does not subsist somewhere outside of the divinity. It is not as though God created—*non de deo sed ex nihilo*—everything from and within a nothingness located outside of "him." If the divine infinity means anything, it renders such an outside impossible. Things can't exist outside of God if God lacks a circumference.

But this infinity does not signify mere immensity. It means also radical intimacy. The apostle Paul conveys this rather precisely in an ancient moment of cross-religious conversation in Athens: this God for whom we search and "grope" is "not far from each one of us. For 'in him we live and move and have our being…'"[19] We all only exist within this divinity—*pan en theos*. Not as within a container, an enclosure, but as within a shared process. All creatures happen within a theos that at the same time flows into all creatures.

Of course intimacy can be confused with identification. When the relational ontology of our entangled differences has been repressed, I am externally related to others, and that history of others within me become simply—me. Without the "connexity" of mutual participation, then the web of life can be torn into fungible units. And of course panentheism can be written off as pantheism—old *Schimpfwort* for a mere identity of pan and God.[20] A metaphysics of substance (Derrida's "presence")—theistic or atheistic—packages the units into separate identities, externally related.

As process theology in its theology and in its activism makes inescapably clear, the alternative to the deadening substantialism requires its own metaphysics. As Whitehead puts the alternative: "Process is the immanence of the infinite in the finite."[21] Here I want to put it this way: all things, pan, come to be in a cosmic intersectionality from which there is no escape— on earth or across the multiverse. If we recognize the living heart of the connectivity as divinity, that heart is the *inmost*, the Latin *intimus*, the intimacy of the infinite.

But—you might reasonably interject—what about James' "finite God" and his influence upon Whitehead? For now it will suffice to say that Whitehead did not take up that bit of James, but shared his resistance to the notion of divine power as control. Whitehead's refusal of God's infinite power—of "his" omnipotence—is key to process theology's liberating theodicy. The reconceptualization of divine agency as entelechic and not efficient causation offers the "divine lure" or "aim" of possibility rather than a causal force of control.

So then the creation unfolds out of a beginningless and endless—infinite—creativity: Whitehead's "primordial nature of God" *calls* the creatures forth, but does not ever simply *cause*. It offers the "lure" or "the initial aim." And what the creature in its moment of becoming—its every moment of genesis—chooses, however unconsciously, will shape the future. For every creature—or actual entity—is a momentary assemblage of the present of its own vast but limited past world. But that present is the future of its past, and in an instant becomes the past of its own future: the present is the real potential of its becoming world. And the divine lure consists of a possibility that remains in itself abstract. It can only become real possibility, and sometimes actuality, through the choices of creatures. And those choices, especially in humans, can be systemically at odds with the lure. The doctrine of original sin does intuit that systemic proclivity, portal of Pandemonium.

The implications for theodicy—and so for practical impact—run deep. For instance I found it helpful as the pandemic hit the US to circulate a pastoral letter (with no language of panentheism, let alone Whitehead). It asked whether God sent the coronavirus as a punishment—like the White House Bible teacher's wrath of God against gays and environmentalists. Or as a lesson or test? Answer: no, no and no; God works otherwise, even in and through a pandemic.

How, then? I have on occasion been at pains to amplify certain biblical resonances with this theology of process. It invites a gospel-tuned attention to the lure of possibility. For instance, the parable of the sower illustrates that lure, that gift of possibility—as seed distributed prodigiously, abundantly, its nurture and its growth depends on its reception. It may be received in shallow mediocrity, in stony indifference or in deep and dark fertility. The sower is neither indifferent nor in control. The sower does not do our work for us.

In other words the divine directionality of the creative process that is the creation itself always takes the form of an invitation, a calling, a "let there be"—of light, of earth, of sea. And the profound cooperativity within the creative process manifests long before humans arrive: "let the earth bring forth…." "Let the sea bring forth…." And the one calling then enjoys—and suffers—the results. In this ancient poetics, read panentheistically, we find no contradiction of scientific truths of cosmic fine-tuning, geological history and biological evolution.[22] Those truths include now strong evidence of human hypercooperativity rather than mere competitive aggression as our evolutionary advantage: a fresh clue to the meaning of the imago dei?[23]

Process theology in its mainly but not exclusively Christian voice does not compete with secular truths. It depends upon them. But as Cobb makes clear it is not the secular but "secularism" which is its own religion, and remains incompatible with any theology. Indeed as Cobb has argued the originators of all the world's so-called religions (he would rather call them Ways) are secularizers—calling their people to transform their world, in their time—their *saeculum*.[24] Through his leadership process theology has been key to the first response of any religion to the sciences of ecology, of climate, of economics. Such a science-tinted genre of progressive theology—however related to the Whiteheadian tradition—supports a politics in which the US president's pan-demonic anti-science in response to climate and now pandemic would be unthinkable. As would be that of the Christian white right wing he so effectively manipulates.

In this sort of context a differently vocalized Christianity may be key to a wide enough solidarity and a deep enough history to sustain resistance, and more—to fuel the *insistence* upon that new world. Such planetary solidarity needs more than external relations between alienated individuals or competing causes, however progressive.[25] It needs the vigorous materialization of a "mutual immanence" that foments creative participation in each other, in each others' worlds. We find ourselves always already entangled with each other—in the otherness of Christianities, of religions, of secularities, of races, of economics and sexes and ages and species. Our entangled difference becomes the resource of an ever renewable and renewing solidarity. Our mutual immanence partakes intimately in an infinite becoming.

The mutuality needs recognition; its theology does not. Except on occasion. And to discern the occasion means to heed the lure. The chance arises amidst any pandemonium—for a more original *daemon*, the *eudaimonia* of the "good spirited" or "flourishing."[26] This is to say, panentheism, by whatever name, helps to stimulate our fragile human hypercooperativity—that gift tragically repressed and repackaged as "we vs them." The conditions of social distancing have revealed both the enlivening potential and the demons of its abuse. Those conditions do not prevent a great uprising against the regnant systems of demonization.

As to the virus: no one knows when the palegreen horse will be put out to pasture; pestilence and other pushbacks of the nonhuman may be just warming up. For all our tangled solidarities, the human may not rise to the occasion. But with the hoofbeats still audible, we are invited even as we invite each other, even very other others—to dance on through the portal.

Acknowledgments

A prior version of the section "Pandemonium city" of this chapter appeared in the blogs ABC and Counterpoint. Thanks to J. D. Mechelke for his editorial assistance.

Notes

1. Revelation 6:7–8, NRSV.
2. Catherine Keller, *Apocalypse After All? Climate, Democracy and Other Last Chances* (New York: Orbis, Forthcoming, 2021).
3. Richard Ostfeld, quoted in John Vidal, "Destroyed Habitat Creates the Perfect Conditions for Coronavirus to Emerge," *Ensia*, republished by *Scientific American* (March 18, 2020).

4 Ibid.
5 Luis P. Villarreal, "Are Viruses Alive?" *Scientific American* (August 8, 2008; originally published December 2004).
6 Alfred North Whitehead, *Process and Reality* (New York: Free Press, 2010), 50. Whitehead is alluding here to William James' "blooming, buzzing world."
7 Title of Lecture VIII in Alfred North Whitehead, *Modes of Thought* (New York: Free Press, 1966), 148.
8 Kathryn Yusoff, *A Billion Black Anthropocenes or None* (Minneapolis: University of Minnesota Press, 2018), 5.
9 Ibid., 107.
10 Ibid., 108.
11 Selena Simmons-Duffin, "White House: Data on Covid-19 and Race Still Weeks Away," *NPR News* (April 20, 2020).
12 Lee Fang, "Trump Cabinet Bible Teacher Blames Coronavirus Pandemic on God's Wrath—Somehow It Involves China, Gay People, and Environmentalists," *The Intercept* (March 24, 2020).
13 Emily Holden, "Michigan: Threat of Toxic Contamination Looms after Dam Failures Trigger Flooding," *The Guardian* (May 20, 2020).
14 Emily Holden, "Climate Science Deniers at Forefront of Downplaying Coronavirus Pandemic," *The Guardian* (April 25, 2020).
15 John Milton, *Paradise Lost* (Originally Published 1667; Chicago: Thompson and Thomas, 1901), 30.
16 Ibid., 28.
17 Ibid.
18 Arundhati Roy, "The Pandemic Is a Portal," *Financial Times* (April 3, 2020).
19 Act 17: 28, *NRSV*.
20 For the best analysis of pantheism and the fear thereof, see Mary Jane Rubenstein, *Pantheologies: Gods, Worlds, Monsters* (New York: Columbia University Press, 2018).
21 Whitehead, *Modes of Thought*, 75.
22 See my *Face of Deep: A Theology of Becoming* (New York: Routledge, 2003).
23 Marcia Pally, "Philosophical Questions and Biological Findings—Part I: Human Cooperativity, Competition, and Aggression," *Zygon* (November 2020). Marcia Pally, *Commonwealth and Covenant: Economics, Politics, and Theologies of Relationality* (Grand Rapids: Eerdmans, 2016), Part II: Chs. 1 and 7.
24 The leading process theologian John B. Cobb, Jr. has written numerous works demonstrating the secular implications and impact of so-called religions. He has worked with prophetic genius to expose the economic drivers of ecological destruction, to which he offers Christian and secular practices of the alternative. *Christ in a Pluralistic Age* (Philadelphia: Westminster, 1975). Herman E. Daly and John B. Cobb Jr., *For the Common Good: Redirecting the Economy toward Community, the Environment, and a Sustainable Future* (Boston: Beacon Press, 1994). *Spiritual Bankruptcy: A Prophetic Call to Action* (Nashville: Abingdon Press, 2010). *Postmodernism and Public Policy: Reframing Religion, Culture, Education, Sexuality,*

Class, Race, Politics, and the Economy (Albany: SUNY series in Constructive Postmodern Thought, 2012).
25 Grace Ji-Sun Kim and Hilda P. Koster, eds., *Planetary Solidarity: Global Women's Voices on Christian Doctrine and Climate Justice* (Minneapolis: Fortress Press, 2017).
26 Thanks to Alex Forrester for suggesting the hook back to the non-demonized ancient daemon.

5 Eschatology in a time of crisis

Sean J. McGrath

In the following chapter, I suggest a pastoral mission for the Church in the midst of the perfect storm of COVID-19, international collapse, and climate change: to draw on her rich resources of eschatological thought to teach the world how to live deliberately and love fiercely when strange new things are beginning and many good things are passing away. The pandemic caused by the coronavirus has compelled us to move more quickly into the future than most of us anticipated or are comfortable with. When the medical/technical fix for COVID-19 finally comes—if it comes—we will emerge from our self-isolation into a fully digitised economy with a largely automated work force. Political strategies that once seemed radical or socialist, such as the universal basic income, now appear necessary to prevent an ever-expanding unemployed precariat from once again precipitating massive health emergencies and economic depressions. The divide between the rich and the poor is becoming even more entrenched, ushering in patterns of visible and accepted inequality not seen since the early nineteenth century. All of these signs of the times raise apocalyptic anxiety and an opportunity for theology to reawaken the eschatological edge of Christian faith.

In the following pages I wish to revisit the psychological and ontological orientation of the eschatological attitude for our troubled times. My assumption is that we do not know how to solve the super-wicked problems of our age, which are all at bottom ecological problems, because we are not only the "late-comers" as Heidegger famously said (*Abendländern*, "occidentals," Westerners or, literally, "evening dwellers") we are also the "new comers," the people of the dawn, which has not yet broken on the horizon.[1] The strategies and practices that will be essential for the ecological civilisation that will survive the end of the Holocene are not only obscure to us; they do not yet exist. At the heart of this chapter are certain technical distinctions, which are often overlooked, between eschatology and teleology, on the one hand, and eschatology and utopian politics, on the other.

I do not mean to suggest that the current situation marks a decisive end of history, or a transition to a final stage of human development. The current situation is not the end of history, even if it *is* the end of the world as most of us who were born in the twentieth century knew it. Clearly a new era of Anthropocenic modernity is beginning. The only reason why this pandemic will be less devastating for humanity than other pandemics (the Spanish Flu, the Bubonic plague) is technology, which has made it possible for states to react swiftly and uniformly to the threat. Technology has allowed our food services to continue, even when billions are forced to shelter-in place. Technology has allowed our financial systems to remain relatively stable, despite record unemployment and the virtual cessation of economic production. For those fortunate enough to work in governance, finance, and the knowledge sector, technology has allowed their work to continue, in some cases more effectively than before. Who knew that all those cell phones would be enough to keep what Deleuze calls "world-integrated capitalism" running?

It is hard to deny that the civilisation that began with the agricultural revolution 12,000 years ago is at a moment of axial shift (not the first and probably not the last). The generation gap between those born prior to the digital age and those born after will be more extreme than any previous generational shift in modern history. No wonder the world lies in the grip of a sense of unstoppable acceleration and irreversible loss. It has been known for some time that we face the imminent end of work through automation. Academic philosophers such as Nick Bostrom seriously consider the prospect of the end of human hegemony on the earth with the rise of artificial intelligence.[2] Noah Yuval Harari speaks of the possibility of a future rule of genetically enhanced humans over those too poor to participate in the collective editing of the human genome.[3] Looming over all of these fears is the prospect of the end of civilisation as such due to the irreversible ecological effects of the carbon legacy of the industrial age. We are understandably unable to imagine how humanity will creatively and morally respond to these signs of the times.

Christians today are under the added burden of having to maintain faith in the face of these impending threats, whether real or imagined, faith that future humans will do better than just survive; they will somehow thrive, for revelation promises us that humanity will persist until the end of time.[4] Divinity and humanity became nondualistically united in Christ for the sake of the redemption of the world, that is, to perfect humanity and through it, to draw all beings into the perfect community of the Trinity.[5] From a Christian perspective, it is unthinkable, therefore, that humanity will be permitted to extinguish itself, despite its best efforts. Christians ought to be adept at dealing with apocalyptic anxiety. Indeed, if previous axial moments in history are any example, the current transition also signals a re-birth of the Church, albeit in a form that may be initially unrecognisable. The eschatological hope which has been the soul of the Church since the first century is anything but quietist, as history has proven; it is an active-passivity, a still and centred making-oneself-available to become the inspired agents for the fundamental changes that must occur.

Reading early Christian eschatology with Heidegger

I will begin with a reflection on a few passages drawn from early Christian literature, beginning with the Epistle of Barnabas, and passing then to Heidegger's justly celebrated reading of Paul.[6] The Epistle of Barnabas was written in Greek in Alexandria between 70 and 132 CE—thus at roughly the same time as the four Gospels. It belongs, with The Book of Revelation, to the class of early Christian writings known as antilegomena, texts that not all Christians accepted as sacred scripture, though many did. The anonymous Epistle was falsely ascribed to Paul's helper Barnabas by both Clement of Alexandria and Origen, which indicates the high regard they had for it. All contemporary scholarship allows us to say of the author is that he or she was an early Christian teacher, who knew some of the oral traditions out of which the Gospels were constructed, and who taught and wrote in Greek during the turbulent times of sporadic Roman persecution which followed the destruction of the Temple and the collapse of Jewish Christianity.

Chapter 4, verse 9 reads:

> Wherefore let us walk circumspectly in these last days. For the entire period of our life and faith will be wasted unless now, in the lawless time and in the impending scandals, we resist as befits God's children.

The phrase "let us walk circumspectly in these last days" is worth reflecting on. The Greek (transliterated) is *dio prosekhōmen en tais eskhatais hēmerais*. There is no reference to "walking" in the Greek, but only a vague suggestion of "holding" oneself (*ekhomen*) with foresight or intention (*pros*).⁷ The translator's somewhat figurative rendering, "walk circumspectly," brings to mind Heidegger's *Being and Time*, and well it should, since the latter is in large part a secularisation of Christian eschatology.⁸ Circumspection (*Umsicht*) in the early Heidegger refers to the fore-theoretical, peripheral sight (*sicht*) typical of everyday being-in-the-world. It is the pre-thematic understanding of a situation characteristic of practical work and dealing with tools. Mechanics and carpenters are adept at it, but circumspection is not a specialisation. As one of Dasein's existentials, circumspection is constitutive of being-in-the-world, as average as the practical know-how deployed in making a cup of tea or opening a door.

Like all Dasein's comportments circumspect concern (*umschtiges Besorgen*) has an inauthentic and an authentic modality.⁹ Average everydayness also knows a mode of circumspection; it deals with the world with a view to fleeing the burden of being. Authentic Dasein by contrast deals circumspectly with the world in "resolute anticipation" of death. Instead of flattening temporality into a manageable homogeneity of indifferent moments that will go on forever, authentic circumspective concern enters fully into the moment of time, into finitude and being-unto-death, transparent to the precarity of the situation, and alive to the finite and concrete possibilities for being-in-the-world that remain. Authentic circumspective concern is deliberative without being controlling, and in its wakefulness remains open to the meaning of the situation. Read through Heidegger, Barnabas is calling his disciples not to remove themselves from the everyday but to enter more deeply into it, and to deal with the things of this world in the anticipation that they are all passing away. The Christians, alongside everyone else, must suffer the turmoil of "the lawless time and the impending scandals." Whatever else these words refer to they speak of the deterioration of a previously stable system of social and political order. They speak of the inevitable decline in civility that such political collapse precipitate ("scandal"), and evoke a general degradation of humanity in the last days. "Barnabas" does not give his disciples a theoretical certainty concerning the end of these trials, nor does he share with them a secret wisdom or esoteric gnosis concerning what is coming, which could comfort them and allay their anxieties. And most importantly, he does not tell them that they should hold themselves aloof from this turmoil, retreating into the soul like a Stoic or an Epicurean. He tells them, rather, that they should "hold forth" and "resist" circumspectly, or carry on deliberately and attentively with whatever they do, paying heed to the signs of the end that are all around them.

The rest of the epistle primarily concerns Barnabas' reading of the signs as fulfilments of Jewish scriptures.

"Circumspect walking" is not aloof or quietist, and and not without stakes. "Barnabas" cannot stress enough the urgency of a proper response to the situation: "For the entire period of our life and faith will be wasted unless now, in the lawless time and in the impending scandals, we resist as befits God's children." The reference to a past to which the disciples are accountable, not the general or universal history of salvation but the intimate, personal history of a specific community, the sense of which depends on what the disciples do now—an "entire period of our life and faith," which risks sinking into nothing and being in vain, wasted, if the disciples fail to rise to the occasion—speaks to the peculiar way that early Christianity lives what Heidegger calls "temporality."[10] Heidegger examined the early Christian eschatological attitude towards time in his 1920–1921 lecture course, *The Phenomenology of Religious Life*.[11] In a now legendary interpretation of Paul's two letters to the Thessalonians, he commented on Paul's account of the Christian life as one of conversion and waiting. For Paul, Heidegger notes, the elect are not distinguished by moral rectitude or by their possession of special knowledge, but by the way they hold themselves in ordinary, daily life (*das Wie des Sich-Verhaltens*). The early Christians are outwardly indistinguishable from other inhabitants of the Greco-Roman world. What makes them Christian is the quality of their attitude, that is, their sobriety, attention, and readiness to meet the demands of the situation. Paul enjoins the Christians to stay awake, to continue to live in a transparently temporal way, always remaining grounded in the decisive event of their "being as having become" (*Gewordensein*), at a certain moment in the past, a new creation, i.e., a Christian. Heidegger notes with interest how Paul commands the Thessalonians to "remember" who they have become in Christ, and calls them back, again and again, to the historical moment of their birth into the Christian community—to continually repeat the moment, while they await the last day.[12]

Heidegger's reading of Paul highlights how active and practically engaged the eschatological attitude truly is. To walk circumspectly is to have a look around, not from a safe theoretical distance, but with our hands in the dirt, to see what is going on *now* from the perspective of one who is intimately involved with it. Christians are to "resist evil" Barnabas says, and hold fast in the trials to come, prepared to lose everything, while still dealing lovingly with others. This paradoxical active-passivity is the heart of genuine eschatological consciousness, and it is as elusive in modern Christian life as it is central to the literature of early Christianity. In his first letter to the Corinthians Paul directly embraces the paradox:

> The appointed time has grown short; from now on, let even those who have wives be as though they had none, and those who mourn as though they were not mourning, and those who rejoice as though they were not rejoicing, and those who buy as though they had no possessions, and those who deal with the world as though they had no dealings with it. For the present form of this world is passing away.[13]

On the one hand, the Corinthians are to practice a degree of total detachment which would earn the admiration of a Theravadin Monk; on the other hand, they will "mourn," "rejoice," "buy," i.e., continue to deal in a lively and loving way with the world. Paul rails against the "idleness" infecting the Thessalonian community, the casual indifference born of a false sense of certainty concerning the end. The enemy of eschatology is not only the secular delusion that this world could be a permanent home for us, but also the religious quietism which neglects what needs to be done here, for the sake of a pseudo, other worldly investment in the next life.[14]

Here is a more contemporary example of what eschatological active-passivity looks like. In late 1961 and early 1962, Gethsemane Abbey, in Kentucky, was bursting at the seams, like other Catholic religious orders, with novices and converts. Soviet-American relations were deteriorating dramatically and reached a nadir of mutual hostility in the Cuban Missile Crisis of October 1962, when the world was as close to nuclear war as it has ever been. In this Abbey at this historical moment, Thomas Merton wrote in his journal of feeling at once overwhelmed with paternal love for the novices entrusted to him as novice master, along with an unshakeable sense that "there is every chance of a disastrous war in the next three to five years."[15] The world was probably bound to end in a nuclear firestorm, and yet it still made sense to welcome young men into the Cistercian novitiate, to help them with their interior struggles, to teach them the Fathers of the Church, and to train them in a long life of monastic service. But did it make human sense? No, and this is the point. Eschatological consciousness calls upon us to live with an understanding of the order of things which can never be fully our own, to live on *borrowed sense*, to trust that things make sense when they plainly don't, which is not to say, to believe just anything, but rather to live fully, but not out of one's own resources, one's own expectations, one's own little plans and small hopes.

From this kind of love necessarily springs hope, hope even for political action, for here, paradoxically, hope is most necessary. Hope is always most necessary precisely where everything, spiritually, seems hopeless. This is precisely in the confusion of politics. Hope against hope that man gradually disarm and cease preparing for destruction and learn at last that he *must* live at peace with his brother.[16]

Two theses on the eschatological attitude: concerning time and justice

The essence of the eschatological attitude can be summed up in two interrelated theses, a first concerning the temporal sense of eschatology, and a second concerning the transcendent quality of eschatological justice. (1) Eschatological time never loops back on itself, as in teleology, but throws us towards an irreversible end (*eschaton*), which cancels the passing forms of this world, even as it renders every event in time singularly and eternally significant, and the moral responsibility of the individual to decide, and so make history, unavoidable and decisive. (2) The eschatological anticipation of the end as the advent of absolute justice places the present under the strictest censure: the world as it exists is unjust and will be condemned as such by what is to come. The two theses contradict respectively the organicism of ancient teleology, and the utopianism of modern revolutionary politics. Both teleology and utopianism assume, in different ways, temporal continuity and final causality. Teleology is the reciprocal and natural determination of the future by the past and the past by the future; utopianism is the political determination of the future by the present. Eschatology, by contrast, is the disruption of the horizonal temporal whole of the past, present, and future by the transcendent.

The first thesis concerns the uni-directedness of time, which stands in marked contrast to the teleological sense of time as cyclical and self-repeating.[17] Eschatology is eventful time, the time in which events can have a singular meaning, and not, by contrast, the time in which events are only meaningful as instantiations of an archetype. In eschatological time, the singular can be meaningful in its singularity, and not, as in teleology, only by virtue of its universality. The moment in teleology is a vanishing mediator of a processively unfolding necessity, as in Hegel. The eschatological event, by contrast, is of "decisive significance," as Kierkegaard put it, by virtue of being once and for all.[18] It is not a part of an organic whole unfolding out of the richness of a beginning, and has no final causal relations with anything that precedes it. Eschatological time is therefore disruptive and revelatory rather than developmental. It is the sudden and alarming unveiling of what Schelling calls the "unprethinkable" (*das Unvordenklich*).[19]

Eschatological time is the time of humanity, and herein lies the secular significance of eschatology for the history of ideas. This is a point that has been driven home by twentieth-century existentialism, which in both its theological and atheist forms depends heavily on the nineteenth-century eschatological turn in biblical studies. By rescuing the singular meaningfulness of certain events (the moment of decision/conversion) from the abyss of past time, and securing the eternal meaning of the contingent, eschatology inaugurates historical thinking. Strictly speaking there is no history without an *eschaton* because there is no true ending to teleological time. The *telos* that fulfils the potencies of the past returns teleological time to the beginning and erases the singularity of the event, validating only the formal or universal meaning of it. Teleological sense is not new but old, not unprecedented but recurrent, participatory, and dependent upon eternal or archetypal pattern. Thus nothing new truly occurs in teleology; rather the everlasting returns again and again in new forms, and time, lacking a genuine end, has no beginning. We are locked in Plato's moving image of eternity, bound to Shiva's wheel of birth, death, and re-birth. The eschatological moment, by contrast, negates what has come before and renders it past in a definitive sense.

Eschatological time is also the time of irrecoverable loss, not the time of fullness, health, and enjoyment, and this is the source of the melancholy that runs as a leitmotif through the Psalms and the Prophets, and even in a certain sense the letters of the New Testament (always qualified by resurrection joy). In eschatological time, "an original message is driven into extremities of oblivion through a series of gradual erasures and ever fainter appearances, which by a logic of reversal, occasion a new dispatch."[20] The point here, somewhat obscured by Caputo's tiresome repetition of the rhetoric of the late Heidegger, is that in eschatological time, something does not come to fruition, as in a teleological development, but dissipates and weakens, until it ends. The last is not the fruition of the potentiality locked in the beginning, not the actualisation, but the running down and running out of the original impulse. This weakening of origins leads to crisis and a longing for a new beginning. The first beginning is lost and over. Eschatological time remembers the beginning, not as that which has come to fruition, but as the promise that was not or is not yet fulfilled. Eschatological time empties itself rather than fills itself; it is "the spending and exhausting of a great beginning."[21]

The second thesis concerns justice (not a point upon which Heidegger can guide us) and underscores the close relationship between eschatological thinking and utopianism. The difference between eschatology and utopian thought is subtle but crucial: both look towards a future that will be different than the past, that is, both are non-teleological; both see the future as the advent of justice, and thus as a judgement on the present and the past. But where eschatology regards the present as constitutively lacking in the means to bring about the desired future, utopianism insists on just the opposite. Utopianism believes above all in humanity and its suppressed potency for justice; it is an essentially modern, Feuerbachian move of reclaiming for humanity all that which was previously projected onto the divine. Utopianism politicises hope and fuses it with the modern will to power. Eschatology, by contrast, believes by virtue of "the absurd," as Kierkegaard put it, that all shall be well. Utopians call for revolution, eschatologists await (but not passively) the coming God. Where the utopian arrogates to the present the capacity to bring justice into presence—invariably at the price of the sacrifice of the innocent—the eschatologist stays with the impossibility of the situation while trusting in the divine will that grounds history. The differences between the two rest on different notions of transcendence; for the utopian the transcendent is the future that has not yet come and which depends upon our taking it upon ourselves as a task; for the eschatologist, the transcendent is the holy, which ultimately is incompatible with the conditions of this world and out of proportion to any social or political power we might possess.[22]

The utopian ultimately turns the holy into the *arche* (ground) of a form of worldly sovereignty, whether this be the sovereignty of a messianic political leader or the sovereignty of a perfected political community. These two attitudes towards justice, the utopian and the eschatological, are so close to one another—contraries rather than opposites—that they are continually cross-fertilising one another and frequently changing places.[23] Eschatologists like Thomas Müntzer become utopians by the slightest shift of emphasis, from divine power as wholly other, to a power immanent in the human, and utopians like the young Dostoevsky become eschatologists through a painful discovery (made in a cell in Siberia) of the inherent fallenness of the human being and the strangeness, the transcendence of earthly sense and conditions, of divine justice. For both utopians and eschatologists, the future is the advent of justice, justice which has never before prevailed on earth, a hope which grounds and legitimatises, even as it intensifies our outrage at the injustices of the present. However, because justice is ontologically deferred by eschatology, not merely displaced to the future, but rendered absolutely transcendent, the present is placed under the stricter censure by the eschatologists. The utopian believes that seeds of the saving power are planted in the present; the eschatologist also believes that divine power is at work in the world, but not as a part of the world, not as a potency of the world, but as that which contradicts the world, and is therefore rejected by the world, summed up in the Hebrew saying, which Jesus used to explain his presence among us, "The stone which the builders rejected has become the cornerstone."[24]

Conclusion

Christians in the age of the perfect storm of pandemic, international collapse, and climate change need to soberly reckon with the end of Christendom.[25] Nostalgia and retreat to liturgical niches will not do. In this destitution, this suffering of the absence of God, Christians are never more Christian, never more followers of the Christ who redeemed the world by losing and becoming lost to the Father. No form of culture or nature is adequate to the revelation. An eschatological community—which is what Jesus founded—never enjoys the security of a teleologically established society. The Church can never be a people nested in a cosmos in which they are at home, or securely set up somewhere near the top of a social-political order. Consequently the eschatological Church will always be tempted to despair that the promise of flourishing ("I came that they might have life, and have it abundantly"[26]) was a lie. But the temptation to despair is the condition of the possibility of hope, hoping against the signs and obvious facts, that the end "will turn itself inside out and become the point of departure for a new beginning."[27]

In sum, the eschatological attitude, which is as relevant in the twenty-first century as it was in the first century of the Common Era, is a paradoxical living for a new world while caring assiduously for this one, and spending oneself tirelessly in service of preserving all that is good, true, and beautiful in it. It is in this caring and not caring,[28] what I have called "eschatological active-passivity," that Christianity hits its stride, in whatever age, and constellates that attitude to time and justice which disrupts the cynicisms, the Gnosticisms, the various forms of nihilism that ran rampant through the Mediterranean world of the first century, and have made a comeback in our own.

Notes

1 See Martin Heidegger, *Early Greek Thinking*, trans. David Farrell Krell and Frank A. Capuzzi (New York, NY: HarperCollins, 1975), 17.
2 Nick Bostrum, "What Happens When Our Computers Get Smarter han We Are?" Ted Talks 2015.

3 Yuval Noah Harari, *21 Lessons for the 21st Century* (New York, NY: Penguin Random House, 2018), Chapter 1.
4 1 Cor 15:28
5 See Rowan Williams, *Christ: The Heart of Creation* (London: Bloomsbury Continuum, 2018).
6 "The Letter of Barnabas," trans. Robert A. Kraft and Jay C. Treat, in Steve Mason and Tom Robinson, eds., *Early Christian Reader. Christian Texts from the First and Second Centuries in Contemporary English Translations* (Peabody, MA: Hendrickson Publishers, 2004), 658–671.
7 Thanks to Memorial PhD student George Saad for this point.
8 See Sean J. McGrath, *The Early Heidegger and Medieval Philosophy: Phenomenology for the Godforsaken* (Washington, DC: Catholic University of America Press, 2006), 185ff.
9 Martin Heidegger, *Being and Time*, trans. John Macquarrie and Edward Robinson (New York, NY: Harper & Row, 1962), 98–100, 403–408.
10 Heidegger, *Being and Time*, Division Two.
11 Martin Heidegger, *The Phenomenology of Religious Life*, trans. Matthias Fritsch and Jennifer Anna Gosetti-Ferencei (Bloomington and Indianapolis: Indiana University Press, 2004).
12 See Heidegger, *Phenomenology of Religious Life*, 66; McGrath, *The Early Heidegger*, 193.
13 1 Cor 7: 29–31
14 2 Thess 3:6–13
15 Thomas Merton, *The Intimate Merton: His Life from His Journals*d. Patrick Hart and Jonathan Montaldo (New YorkNY: HarperCollins, 1999), 193.
16 Ibid., 191.
17 See for example Plato's thesis of time as the moving image of eternity in the *Timaeus* (37d), which is the prototype for Aristotle's teleology, or the Vedantic notion of time as samsara. The cyclical nature of time is also a fundamental theme of ancient Chinese thought (notably in Taosim, where it is described as the Tao that can be named (by distinction from the nameless Tao), and "the mother of the ten thousand things" [*The Complete Tao Te Ching*, trans Gia-Fu Feng and Jane English (Vintage Books, 1989) stanza 1].
18 Søren Kierkegaard, *Philosophical Fragments / Johannes Climacus*, ed. and trans. Howard v. Hong and Edna H. Hong (Princeton University Press, 1985), 13
19 F.W.J. Schelling, *Philosophy of Revelation*, trans. Klaus Ottmann (Thompson, Spring Publications, 2020), 124.
20 John Caputo, *Radical Hermeneutics: Repetition, Desconstruction, and the Hermeneutic Project* (Bloomington and Indianapolis: Indiana University Press, 1987), 160.
21 Ibid., 161.
22 See Saitya Brata Das, *The Political Theology of Kierkegaard* (Edinburgh University Press, 2020), 4.
23 Ernst Bloch, *The Principle of Hope*, three Volumes, trans Neville Plaice, Stephen Plaice, Paul Knight (MIT Press, 1995).
24 Ps 118:22; Mat 21:42.
25 In this regard I suggest revisiting the works of death-of-God theologian, Thomas Altizer, particularly his later, less known writings. See Lissa

McCullough, "Apocalypticism as Political Theology," Critical Essay #10 in "Thomas J. J. Altizer & Radical Theology," special issue of *Journal for Cultural and Religious Theory* 18, no. 4 (Winter 2019), guest edited by Lissa McCullough.
26 Jn 10:10.
27 Caputo, *Radical Hermeneutics*, 161.
28 "Teach us to care and not to care. Teach us to sit still." T.S. Eliot, *Ash Wednesday* (London: Faber & Faber, 1930), VI.

6 The multidimensional unity of life, theology, ecology, and COVID-19

Derek A. Michaud

Introduction

The COVID-19 pandemic is a multidimensional crisis. The SARS-CoV-2 virus itself represents the most obvious aspect, of course, and we are rightly occupied with measures to avoid, limit the spread, and eliminate it from surfaces and bodies. Yet as we engage in social distancing, face mask-wearing, thorough hand washing, and other measures additional dimensions of the crisis are illuminated too. For example, the global economy with its near-instantaneous transportation of goods, people, and viruses around the world; the successes and failures of political systems to protect human health; the morality of health precautions for the benefit of others including the most vulnerable among us; the psychological effects of massive illness, death, and social isolation; the pedagogical impacts of disruptions in school routines. The racial and socioeconomic disparities in rates of infection and mortality too shine a light on the fact that all was not well before the pandemic. Likewise, after the virus is tamed by behavior and vaccine many of the dimensions of the current crisis will remain with us without specific remediation. As we work through the direct challenge of COVID-19, the opportunity exists to revisit the way we frame all these issues and more. In this chapter, I suggest a possible way forward that embraces Paul Tillich's theological vision of life as a multidimensional unity. This vision, I argue, is more adequate conceptually and provides the needed motivation for the long-term action of remaking ourselves and our world toward the flourishing of all.

The multidimensionality of the COVID-19 crisis can be seen perhaps most clearly in how every intervention results in countless effects many of which are deeply undesirable. For example, social isolation or quarantine while essential for containing the spread of the virus is associated worldwide with emotional disturbance, depression, insomnia, and "post-traumatic stress symptoms."[1] Undoubtedly, such psychological distress is preferable to the alternative of more lives lost to the coronavirus. Yet, these too are failures to achieve adequate human health. Inherently social animals, we cannot thrive in hermetically sealed isolation.[2] Moreover, even as we pin our hopes on a vaccine the possibility, though not necessity, remains that these interventions will spur new viruses to develop setting us on the path of a "high-stakes game of whack-a-mole."[3] Without significant thought and sustained dialogue about all the ways viruses pass to us from non-human animals, and between each other, a vaccine may not be the panacea many hope for, to say nothing of the potential for inequalities of access to such medicine along predictable lines. In all these ways and more, we find that when we push on any one aspect of our current crisis, we find innumerable additional considerations immediately follow. The COVID-19 pandemic is multidimensional to its core.

Yet, we consistently tend toward simple monodimensional answers. Partly this is understandable since our sciences work by isolation of variables and analysis. We come to understand even novel viruses like the current scourge remarkably well and quickly this way. But the challenge posed by the virus is not merely biochemical as we have seen. Even when medical research discovers a way to eliminate the virus, we will still be faced with questions that cannot be answered in scientific terms alone. Where, when, and how to vaccinate for COVID-19 will raise moral, political, cultural, and religious issues as well. We come to know biology analytically in controlled environments, but our lives are lived synthetically in uncontrolled environments full of ambiguity and uncertainty. Life is synthetic in the sense that emergent unities arise out of diversities without eliminating or being reducible to them. Our psyches arise out of but are not simply reducible to the physical-chemical and metabolic dimensions of ourselves. In short, not only do we live in complex webs of interrelations with others and our environment, we ourselves are web-like.

To promote human flourishing in the face of the pandemic two things are needed. First, if we are to make real sustained progress an adequate conception of ourselves and our challenges is required. While primarily a psychological category, I take flourishing to lie at the conjunction of health or well-being in all dimensions of life from the inorganic, through the biological and psychological, into the spiritual and historical. Only with conceptual clarity and accuracy can we hope for effective policy and cultivation leading to flourishing. Second, grounds for motivation are needed to sustain action over time. Multidimensional remediation is extremely challenging. Without metaphysical grounds for hope, it is all too easy to see our inevitable failures along the way as merely engineering or technical failings prompting us to redouble our efforts to fix things monodimensionally. But, as has already been suggested, we cannot ultimately address our ills in this piecemeal fashion. Our failures to provide for public health already involve failures of the heart and spirit too. If we would seek true human welfare, we must work on all fronts simultaneously. Fortuitously, the Christian theological tradition of reflection on *salvation* and eschatological consummation has always included this expansive notion of health (*salus*).

To the extent that they register the multidimensional unity of life other religious traditions may also provide the necessary framing and motivation. The dharmic traditions of India have long understood the interdependence of all things as illustrated, for example, by the Buddhist concept of Pratītyasamutpāda.[4] Indigenous traditions from around the world also appreciate the fundamental truth of the unity of all things under spirit, for example, the "Great Spirit" Wakan Tanka among the Lakota of North America.[5] All these and more should be listened to and learned from on these issues. Since one must speak from somewhere however, I take up my topic here employing selected resources out of the Greek philosophical and Christian theological traditions.

By framing the multidimensional unity of life within a transcendent horizon, we open the conceptual space to attend to and act for the flourishing of ourselves and our world. In contrast, conceiving of the world of finite things and their relations as the whole of reality without reference to the ecstatic Ground thereof risks missing its non-reductive unity. As David Bentley Hart has put it, "Any ultimate ground of explanation must be one that unites all dimensions of being in a simpler, more conceptually parsimonious principle."[6] We best attend to the immensity and complexity of the challenges facing our spatiotemporal world by framing it in terms of the creative Ground that both supports and exceeds it. We gain the ability to grasp ourselves and our world by first being grasped by the Divine, not as another in the cavalcade of creation but as the very ground thereof—distinct from the many yet closer to each than they are to themselves.[7] Indeed, our attempts to reduce the diversity of our world and its challenges to any single dimension of reality amount to a kind of idolatrous misidentification of the ground of the unity and therefore existence of the cosmos. The One presupposed by the many in our world cannot be a member of that plurality nor can it be separate from it either.[8] In the language of religious symbols, by viewing all things in light of their common source and hope in God we understand the nature of our predicament and find the strength to be healed.

The multidimensional unity of life

The "multidimensional unity of life" is Tillich's way of describing the actuality of being as "life" in an ontological sense, including organic and non-organic dimensions.[9] By "dimension" Tillich means those aspects of reality commonly called "levels" such as physical, chemical, biological, social, and historical. He identifies localized centers of integration among dimensions as "realms." A dominant dimension determines the character of these centers.[10] For example, the chemical processes in the human body, which are often identical or very similar to those in other organisms, represent a dimension and the individuals as centers of awareness and agency in the psychological and moral dimensions are a realm within which such processes take place. Tillich employs the language of dimensions to avoid the misleading qualities of "level" talk. Unlike levels, dimensions allow us to register the relationships without subjecting the lower to the supremacy of the higher. Dimensions more accurately represent how aspects of the actuality of being are in non-reductive and non-competitive interrelation with each other. Above all, this is key for Tillich to a proper understanding of God as the Ground of Being rather than a "highest being" among others.[11] As Rowan Williams has put it in commenting on Augustine of Hippo,

> God's action cannot *compete* with created agency, God does not have to overcome a rival presence, the creative power of God is not power exercised unilaterally over some other force, but is itself the ground of all power and all agency within creation.[12]

Tillich next addresses the dynamics of life. "All life processes involve a movement from self-identity to self-alteration, and a return to one's self in such a way that three functions can be recognized in them: self-integration, self-creation and self-transcendence."[13] All three functions are properly predicated of human agents but not in an absolute or autonomous sense. All presuppose the creative Ground from whence all things come.[14] Behind his intentionally twentieth-century language of psychoanalysis and existentialism, Tillich affirms the ancient philosophy of participation. For him, to be at all is to participate in Being and God is Being itself beyond the distinction between essence and existence.[15] This unconditioned abysmal conception of God transcends the finitude of mere beings and is experienced by humanity as the true and the good which point to the Ground of all being as Being itself.[16] Just as it is by participation that we exist (God as Ground) so too do we find our final aim in God as Spirit, symbol of fully essentialized being, the goal of the human spirit in the New Being.[17] God is Spirit because God is the "unity of the ontological elements and the *telos* of life."[18] In short, it is in God that "we live and move and have our being."[19] When open to the theonomous depths of our essential being in and through the symbol of Jesus as the Christ, we experience the New Being, being remade in the image of the living God, becoming who we always were essentially and overcoming estrangement from our Ground.[20] The processes of growth, theotic healing, and the emergence of new non-reducible dimensions extends to all beings and are only most obvious in humanity because in us all dimensions are always actually present. Thus, the multidimensional unity of life points to an essential state of harmonious communion of all things with themselves, each other, and their ground in God. This harmony is an ontological potentiality and normative ideal only ambiguously realized within existence before the eschaton.[21]

The world is thus an ontological process within which the actualization of any one dimension or realm presupposes the actualization of those that precede them.[22] For example, the chemical dimension is reliant on, and a transcendent effect of, the dimension of the physical (i.e., physics). The same structure of emergent self-transcendence applies to all the dimensions of life and human life unites them all in a centered whole leading by grace to abundant life in the Spirit.[23]

Considerations of health, well-being, and human flourishing as the spiritual essentialization of existence provide perhaps the clearest illustration of the multidimensional unity of life. "In order to speak of health, one must speak of all dimensions of life."[24] Tillich argues that the various aspects of reality "are present within each other and do not lie alongside or above each other."[25] All participate in God as the Ground of Being. Tillich distinguishes seven dimensions in "The Meaning of Health" (mechanical, chemical, biological, psychological, mental, spiritual, and historical), but notes that these are not exhaustive but are merely expedient for discussion chosen out of innumerable dimensions. In human beings all the dimensions of life are present.[26]

Tillich discusses human health in terms of the dimensions of life he has identified as present in and indeed composing humanity.[27] In the mechanical dimension human "health is the adequate functioning of all the particular parts of man. Disease is the non-functioning of these parts because of incidents, infections, and imbalances. Healing, then, is the removal of the diseased parts or their mechanical replacement: surgery."[28] Under the chemical dimension health is "the balance of chemical substances and processes."[29] Neither of these two types of healing is complete on their own however. Each requires the other as well as the more inclusive dimension of the biological where ideally "balance is achieved between self-alteration and self-preservation."[30] The biological dimension involves the health of the entire organism and it leads to the dimension of self-awareness in which the dialectical processes of life are most clearly visible. Psychological health involves "self-alteration in every moment, in receiving reality, in mastering it, in being united with parts of it, in changing it, etc." and "in all this a risk is involved" which "accounts for the reluctance to take all these encountered pieces of reality into one's centered self" which leads to neurotic withdrawal from reality.[31]

The spiritual dimension designates life in meaning and value as expressed in morality, culture, and religion. In this dimension "the problem of health receives another depth and breadth, which then, conversely, is decisive for all the preceding dimensions."[32] In addition to considerations needed for mere survival and continued living, with the spiritual dimension health and healing are raised to the register of flourishing by actualizing domains of value that are explicitly about meaning, purpose, and community. Morality, for example, involves "the self-actualization of the person in his centered encounter with the other."[33] Moral healing involves "the power of overcoming both distortions [of legalism and lawlessness]" and for this to be accomplished

> the [human] spirit must be grasped by something which transcends it, which is not strange to it, but within which is the fulfillment of its potentialities. It is called 'Spirit' (with a capital S). Spirit is the presence of what concerns us ultimately, the ground of our being and meaning.[34]

While Tillich maintains that spiritual healing is the only kind which is effected "directly" (that is, with minimal mediation) by the Spiritual Presence, he also says that *any healing*, under any dimension and in any realm, is ultimately the product of the divine healing power symbolized in the New Being.[35] This affirmation of the cosmic scope of salvation has been a particular emphasis of the Eastern Orthodox tradition and reflects some of the earliest Christian thinking on the significance of the work of God in Christ and the Holy Spirit.[36] Indeed, the notion that salvation extends to the natural world in the eschaton is even found in scripture.[37]

The spiritual dimension with its explicit reference to culture as a bearer of spirit and the Spiritual Presence as a healing force leads Tillich to the dimensions of history and society. In this regard, his question is "To what degree is personal health possible in a society which is not a 'sane society' (Erich Fromm)?"[38] In response, Tillich offers the idea of simply building a sane society is not an adequate answer because it ignores the ambiguities inherent in history and the necessity of health among members of society.[39] In his extensive discussion of the historical dimension in volume three of the *Systematic Theology* Tillich answers this question with the symbol of the Kingdom of God, an eschatological vision both temporal and eternal which finds its realization in the "eternal now."[40] Consequently, Tillich concludes, "The road through the many dimensions, and the meaning of health within them, has shown ... that complete healing includes healing under all dimensions."[41]

Ecology in multidimensional perspective

Tillich took with radical seriousness "the notion that nature shares with humanity the fundamental experience of estrangement or, in mytho-poetic biblical terms, of 'fallenness'" and accordingly the non-human has an important place in Tillich's soteriology and eschatology.[42] Indeed, he saw all of reality in essentially the same terms as his analysis of human beings.[43] Thus, all dimensions of life that are present in humanity undergo the transition from essence to existence which brings about our hubris, concupiscence, and sin as well as ambiguity in the dynamics of life.[44] As a result, Tillich extends the diagnosis of the predicament of existential estrangement from essential being to all of nature. As creatures, we exist as pale imitations of our true selves. While made for harmonious communion with ourselves, our world, and our Ground, our existential predicament is to realize our essential natures only ambiguously. Yet, for all our estrangement we are not, and could not be, separate from ourselves, our world, and God. "Man reaches into nature, as nature reaches into man. They participate in each other and cannot be separated from each other."[45] Therefore, Tillich saw "the assault on the non-human world" as an attack on "the interdependent fabric that unifies all life, from the biological to the cultural" as well as the spiritual and the historical.[46] Thus, the "health" of nature is affected by humanity, and humanity is affected by the health of nature too.

The clearest statements of Tillich's multidimensional vision of the health of all reality are made in connection with the New Being.[47] As Drummy notes, Tillich's "entire theory of redemption rests on the conviction that 'there is no salvation of man if there is no salvation of nature, because man is in nature and nature is in man'."[48] Salvation then consists of the cosmic healing of all creatures.[49] Indeed, it is Tillich's qualified anti-anthropocentrism that has most attracted the attention of recent ecotheologians.[50]

Tillich's implicit theology of nature is well suited to address the contemporary conflicts between ecological stewardship and human well-being. Instead of promising a return to Eden and the utopian communion of all living beings with each other, his thought recognizes the inherent struggles associated with life. Tillich offers the promising vision of a world that is always struggling to balance the demands of its inhabitants and the various dimensions of life present in them toward a goal of manifesting our essential natures in existence. The dimensions of life are united even when they are in different realms (e.g., human beings or trees). Estrangement from nature, like estrangement from our essential selves, affects our overall well-being in all dimensions too. Our misuse of nature diminishes its health in all its dimensions as well, including potentially the spiritual dimension.[51]

On Tillich's view, then, salvation includes rocks, stars, plants, and animals as well as human beings. As the only beings who actualize the spiritual dimension and with it morality it is we human beings who bear responsibility, guilt, and the full depth of the effects of estrangement and its healing in the New Being and Spiritual Presence.[52] While Tillich affirms the shared status of "fallenness" (existential estrangement) for all creatures human beings are responsible for "the Fall." As moral agents, we have an obligation to make things right, though without the New Being borne by the symbol of Jesus as the Christ our attempts ultimately fail.[53] We are therefore responsible for the ontological health of all things by our freedom to act and our status as deciding selves that unite the dimensions.

Pandemic in multidimensional perspective

History amply shows that major crises are always also spiritual crises. As Tillich suggests this is because life is pregnant with spiritual potential everywhere and especially focused around the actualization of human life. For all the justified criticisms of Lynn White's famous thesis about the origins of modern ecological crises in varieties of Christian dominion over nature on at least one point he surely hit the mark.[54] Religious values and motivations matter profoundly for our relationship to non-human nature. In our current pandemic, this has become tragically clear in examples of religiously motivated disregard for public health measures. From Greek Orthodox bishops claiming that disease cannot be spread by Holy Communion to conservative American

Christians defying quarantine orders, misguided theology has led to illness and unnecessary loss of life.[55]

Predictably, the more vocal opponents of religion have seized upon these examples to heap scorn on faith while ignoring the mainstream acceptance of public health measures by individual Christians and their church communities. But the answer, as White pointed out, to bad theology which brings death is good theology that fosters life. While easy to dismiss as the stuff of sentimentality and garden decorations, White's suggestion that Christians embrace the spirituality of St. Francis of Assisi is entirely consistent with the implicit theology of nature developed by Tillich, who placed his theological work within the "Augustinian-Franciscan" tradition of Christian Platonism.[56]

By viewing the multidimensional unity of life in terms of participation in the Divine Life, Tillich points beyond the views rightly condemned by White and others.[57] In place of a theology of dominance over nature, a vision of true flourishing opens that rightly situates human beings in our ecological embeddedness while recognizing the value of the spiritual dimension in us including culture, religion, and history.[58]

Just as Tillich's pneumatology explains the failure of purely instrumental and anthropocentric approaches to ecology to foster true flourishing, so too does it point the way toward more accurate and productive reflection on the current pandemic. The multidimensional framework allows us to register, discuss, and respond to the ontologically interdependent challenges in our world without reducing them to consideration under a single metric. As mentioned at the outset of this chapter, measures that work well for biochemical problems like viral transmission and infection may not be ideal for maintaining mental health. Approaches meant to maximize economic efficiency ("reopening the economy") may contribute to physical illness that is even more disruptive over time. Structures and institutions, manifestations of our spiritual dimension as moral, cultural, and political beings, that lead to the flourishing of some may unjustly accomplish their task at the expense of others. If we are to seek the flourishing of all we require a framework that can resist the temptation to view the dimensions of life as competitors and that allows us to appreciate how the actualization of potential in each and all of us is integrally rooted in the actualization of all the rest. An approach to life in all its complexity, ambiguity, and struggle that resists the totalization and homogenization of multiplicity while appreciating the fundamental unity of all as creatures.

The multidimensional unity of life as understood by Tillich provides just such an approach by recognizing the truth of what so many of us have realized instinctively during this pandemic; we truly are in this together. But we are always already in this together. For that is what it means to be a living being. Moreover, we human beings as realized centers of agency and relationship actualizing all the dimensions of life self-consciously are likewise in this with all the other creatures too. Your flourishing is not separable from that of your environment and the social forces that shape both. Our flourishing is not separable from yours, mine, and ultimately the world's.

Our interconnectedness does not absolve us of the responsibility to make difficult choices about how best to seek the potential of all. Yet, as a map, the multidimensional unity of life can truly tell us where to turn only if we know where we want to go. As theology though it is suffused already with normative assumptions about the good life rooted in the Divine Life. To fully adopt the framework is to opt to inhabit an imaginary at once totally committed to the here and now and an eschatological future neither fully known nor fully of our making. To love ourselves and our creaturely neighbors fully means opening to and accepting the transformative power of the Ground of all Being.

Toward a public theology of multidimensional health

In Genesis, we are told that humanity is created in the image of God. In us, a unique degree of the Divine Life is made manifest. In us, the world has a creature who can decide the fate not only of itself but of all beings. Yet, it is from the inorganic dust of the ground that we were formed and on the same day that the earth is bidden to bring forth living creatures.[59] We are, as it were, firsts among equals as creatures under the creator of all. Tillich's multidimensional unity of life more accurately and hopefully shows us in our true place, all talk of "dominion" notwithstanding. By attending to the needs of all under heaven, in all their dimensions, secure in the hope of the recreative power of God may we finally take our place as wardens of each other and our fellow creatures.

Notes

1 Samantha K. Brooks et al., "The Psychological Impact of Quarantine and How to Reduce It: Rapid Review of the Evidence," *The Lancet* 395 (2020): 912–920, 913. https://doi.org/10.1016/S0140-6736(20)30460-8.
2 Aristotle, *Politica*, ed., William David Ross (Oxford: Oxford University Press, 1957), 1253a7-11.
3 Melinda W. Moyer, "Vaccines Are Pushing Pathogens to Evolve," *Quanta Magazine*, 10 May 2018, https://www.quantamagazine.org/how-vaccines-can-drive-pathogens-to-evolve-20180510/.

4 Peter Harvey, "The Conditioned Co-Arising of Mental and Bodily Processes within Life and between Lives," in *A Companion to Buddhist Philosophy*, ed., Steven M. Emmanuel (Hoboken, NJ: Wiley-Blackwell, 2013), 37–68.
5 Julian Rice, *Before the Great Spirit: The Many Faces of Sioux Spirituality* (Albuquerque: University of New Mexico Press, 1998).
6 David B. Hart, *Theological Territories: A David Bentley Hart Digest* (Notre Dame: Notre Dame University Press, 2020), 127.
7 Augustine, *Confessions*, 3.6.11; Nicholas of Cusa, *De Li Non Aliud*.
8 Paul Tillich, *Systematic Theology*, 3 vols (Chicago, IL: University of Chicago Press, 1951, 1957, 1963), I: 235–289. Hereafter ST.
9 ST III: 11. My discussion of multidimensional unity of life here revisits reflections that appeared in "Health as a Metaphor for the Created Condition," *Bulletin of the North American Paul Tillich Society* 31, no. 2 (Spring 2005): 28–44.
10 ST III: 11–30. Also, Tillich's "Dimensions, Levels, and the Unity of Life," in *Main Works/Hauptwerke*, ed., Gert Hummel (Berlin; New York: De Gruyter, 1992), 6: 401–416.
11 ST III: 12–15.
12 Rowan Williams, *On Augustine* (London: Bloomsbury Continuum, 2016), 72.
13 Eduardo Cruz, "On the Relevance of Paul Tillich's Concept of Life," in *Paul Tillich's Theological Legacy: Spirit and Community*, ed., Frederick J. Parrella (Berlin; New York: De Gruyter, 1995), 118–124, 122.
14 ST III: 31.
15 ST I: 205. Also, Douglas Hedley, "Tillich and Participation," in *Returning to Tillich: Theology and Legacy in Transition*, eds., Russell Re Manning and Samuel Shearn (Berlin: De Gruyter, 2017), 31–40.
16 ST I: 206–207.
17 Ibid., 244–249.
18 Ibid., 249.
19 Acts 17: 28.
20 ST II: 96, 125–135.
21 ST III: 15.
22 Ibid., 16.
23 Ibid., 42, 254, 256.
24 Paul Tillich, "The Meaning of Health," *Perspectives in Biology and Medicine* 5, no. 1 (1961): 92–100, 92.
25 Tillich, "Meaning," 94.
26 Ibid.
27 Ibid., 96–99.
28 Ibid., 95.
29 Ibid., 96.
30 Ibid.
31 Ibid., 96–97.
32 Ibid., 97. Also ST III: 111–282.
33 Tillich, "Meaning," 97.
34 Tillich, "Meaning," 98. Also ST III: 111–114.
35 ST III: 275; ST II: 96.

36 See, e.g., Andrew Louth, "The Cosmic Vision of Saint Maximus the Confessor," in *In Whom We Live and Move and Have Our Being: Panentheistic Reflections on God's Presence in a Scientific World* (Grand Rapids; Cambridge: Eerdmans, 2004), 184–196; John Chryssavgis, *Creation as Sacrament: Reflections on Ecology and Spirituality* (London: T & T Clark, 2019).
37 E.g., Acts 3: 21; Romans 8: 18–30; Ephesians 1: 8–10.
38 Tillich, "Meaning," 98–99.
39 Ibid., 99.
40 ST III: 297–423.
41 Tillich, "Meaning," 99.
42 Michael F. Drummy, *Being and Earth: Paul Tillich's Theology of Nature* (Lanham, MD: University Press of America, 2000), 35.
43 Drummy, *Being and Earth*, 78, 82–92.
44 Ibid., 80. Also Cruz, "Tillich's Concept of Life," 120–122; ST I: 163–210, ST II: 19–96, ST III: 11–110, 300–361.
45 ST II: 43.
46 Drummy, *Being and Earth*, 62.
47 ST II: 95.
48 Drummy, *Being and Earth*, 87.
49 Ibid., 90. Also Pan-chui Lai, "Paul Tillich and Ecological Theology," *The Journal of Religion* 79, no. 2 (1999): 233–249.
50 Abbey-Anne Smith, *Animals in Tillich's Philosophical Theology* (London: Palgrave Macmillan, 2017), 199–233; Keith Ka-fu Chan, *Life as Spirit: A Study of Paul Tillich's Ecological Pneumatology* (Berlin; Boston, MA: De Gruyter, 2018).
51 ST III: 276.
52 Drummy, *Being and Earth*, 83.
53 ST II: 39–41, 80–86.
54 Lynn White, "The Historical Roots of Our Ecologic Crisis," *Science* 155, no. 3767 (10 March 1967): 1203–1207. On reception see Elspeth Whitney, "Lynn White Jr.'s 'the Historical Roots of Our Ecologic Crisis' after 50 Years," *History Compass* 13, no. 8 (August 2015): 396–410.
55 Yiannis Baboulias, "Communion and the Coronavirus: COVID-19 Triggers Deep Orthodox Divisions," *Balkan Investigative Reporting Network*, 27 April 2020, https://balkaninsight.com/2020/04/27/communion-and-the-coronavirus-covid-19-triggers-deep-orthodox-divisions/; Jonathan Merritt, "Some of the Most Visible Christians in America Are Failing the Coronavirus Test," *The Atlantic*, 24 April 2020, https://www.theatlantic.com/ideas/archive/2020/04/christian-cruelty-face-covid-19/610477/.
56 John P. Dourley, *Paul Tillich and Bonaventure: An Evaluation of Tillich's Claim to Stand in the Augustinian-Franciscan Tradition* (Leiden: Brill, 1975).
57 ST III: 107–110, 134–138, 155–161, 268–271, 280, 291–294.
58 ST III: 25–30.
59 Genesis 1: 24–27. Thanks to John Chryssavgis for the observation.

7 Between catastrophes
God, nature and humanity
John Milbank

Introduction

The coronavirus pandemic has the nature of a genuine 'event' insofar as its reality is in excess of our attempts fully to account for it as to origins, causes, extent or implications. Nevertheless, just how epochal an event it will prove is not so certain. For some commentators, it remains simply a temporary interruption, legitimately requiring an extraordinary but temporary response. For others, it is a sign of a much larger and ongoing ecological crisis. Both these groups tend to welcome a current return to greater levels of state action and public cooperation. But for still others this extraordinary response is not to be regarded as either just provisional or benign, but as an intensification of existing and sinister political economic processes, tending to both surveillance and mutual isolation.

This contrast is somewhat echoed in terms of spiritual and religious assessments of our current predicament. For many people, the pandemic is a warning of our disordered human relationship to life on earth; but for dissenters the response to it already implies an overvaluing of life as such which so excessively foregoes risk as to endanger our living of truly worthwhile and meaningful lives, perhaps in preparation for a greater life beyond death.

Let us briefly consider these three controverted dimensions of our current global situation: how truly significant is this crisis? Is it the end of neoliberalism or the intensification of tyranny in the name of emergency? And are we now putting life before money, or instead replacing the risky pursuit of a truly human existence with a calculus of death limitation?

Between catastrophes

First, is it true that 'nothing will ever be the same again', or is this just a long drawn-out hiatus?[1] In a sense this is an old-fashioned occurrence: there have been many pandemics throughout history and this one is comparatively mild. They are just bolts from the blue, merely metaphorical 'attacks' by banal natural agents lacking in all meaning. COVID-19 is the latest in a series of relatively mild modern plagues whose effect is indeed severe but nonetheless passing. It may intensify certain existing trends towards digitalisation and working from home, and increase the abasements endured by those workers who cannot do that—but that is all. No one seriously saw this coming and the measures taken against the pandemic are just pragmatic, akin to the measures taken in wartime. A political switch to Keynesian tactics does not therefore indicate any permanent alteration and these tactics have been deployed to defend local capitalism in the face of the suspension of some global linkages. The financial sector has still been prioritised and workers have only been assisted to the degree that the market cannot sustain a total collapse in demand beyond a certain level.

To a degree, Bruno Latour confirms this view by arguing that the coronavirus crisis is not a 'dress rehearsal' for coming ecological apocalypse.[2] Again, it is too old-fashioned for that, as we can see by the fact that it has reinvigorated the role of the nation state and modes of 'biopolitical' control at work ever since the year 1800. Governments have deliberately sought to play the selectively medical role of extending some lives, while they have 'economised' the worth of others which are seen as sacrificially indispensable to the running of the economy and to the sustaining of human life in general. What is more, a typically modern duality of culture versus nature has also been re-invoked: we are supposedly in human solidarity against an alien natural force with which we are 'at war'. But the deeper ecological crisis threatening all 'habitation' of the earth which we face is not like this. It is first of all a far more general threat which cannot be handled by national agencies alone and which civil society has not as yet given governments 'the permission' to handle.[3] Second in this instance it is as if human beings are the 'virus' threatening nature, although nature includes themselves. Just for this reason, meeting this more general threat requires a questioning of the nature versus culture divide.

On this view then, the crisis might not change things as much as we think, and it is not all that obviously in a continuum with ecological crisis in general. There are reasons both to heed this double caution and somewhat to qualify it. Although no one could have predicted this pandemic in its precise instance, experts have in fact been warning about the likelihood of pandemics of this kind for years and governments have been variously preparing for them. Moreover, recent novel viruses, including this one, cannot merely be seen as acts of God. To the contrary, they usually involve a jumping from wild animals to humans and this has been made more likely by human activity, including human penetration into the wild, and the economic reach of globalisation. Therefore, as Latour himself stresses, the pandemic cannot without obfuscation be understood in terms of a nature versus culture duality. We are not really threatened just by a biological agent; it is only an aberrant agent because its agency is compounded by many levels of human agency both individual and accidental and networked and habitual.

For this reason, and also because there are likely to be other pandemics in the future, we cannot be sure, even at the merely 'natural' level, whether this crisis is here to stay or not. It has indeed both features of a traditional plague and others related to a more recent disordering of human interactions with the natural world. Even if more specifically ecological threats are somewhat different, the current crisis already presents some of the dilemmas that those threats will pose far more acutely: how to balance the need for collective action with the sustaining of human freedom? How to achieve at once a pragmatically needed devolution of action and responsibility to local level and at the same time increase an equally required global coordination and solidarity? How can the state acquire both the habits and the legitimacy to mediate between these two poles? How do we balance the need for immediate employment with the longer-term one for permacultures: an issue that can divide workers from each other? How to integrate human dignity with natural equilibrium? How to balance survival with what survival is for?

Between politics

The second question is: how are we to assess the political responses to the 'great pause' in our current lives? We should surely welcome the fact of an increase in human solidarity, even if or perhaps all the more because it has to be exercised sacrificially through human isolation.[4] It is good that there proves to be a limit to the human tolerance of utilitarian economism. Thus hardly anyone agrees with Giorgio Agamben's semi-conspiratorial view that COVID-19 was just a particularly virulent flu bug which has occasioned an excessive reaction designed to suspend all normal procedures in the name of a permanent rule by exception.[5] Though nothing like as dangerous as some once thought, it is nonetheless sufficiently so as to justify the emergency measures taken, unless one has adopted a callous disregard for human existence.

However, the view that the crisis indeed provides both for the State and for Capital a convenient suspension of the usual norms is far more plausible. In circumstances of lockdown, the power of the digital giants and of the online retailers has been greatly increased. The same applies to the reinforcement of home-working which, by isolating workers from shared solidarity, tends to increase their controllability from afar. This can operate as a covert proletarianisation of the professional and lower managerial classes: submitting them more and more to routine procedure. At the same time, the leverage of outdoor workers is not necessarily going to be increased: given the spur of much increased unemployment and the militarised disaggregation and de-unionisation also of these workers, the very opposite may ensue.

What is more, despite arguments about the relative virtues of suppression versus herd immunity and of balancing immediately threatened lives versus sustaining the economy, in the end all governments are likely to adopt a mixing of both strategies and to attempt some sort of such balance. If we wanted instead to mitigate these difficult choices, we would have to switch to a totally different political and economic order.

In particular, we would have to revisit the entire question of what work is for and how the goals of personally fulfilling and socially beneficial work might require different balances of working alone and together in direct physical proximity. We would have to consider how comprehensively to minimise outdoor dangers, to compensate for them and to provide a real and generous bedrock of security for those threatened with a more precarious existence, including unemployment. Indeed, we would try to remove that precariousness and insecurity entirely by fully recognising the equal social importance and difficulty of more 'basic' tasks like building, transporting, serving and caring. We would come to see that these are 'arts' also and we would seek to render them more so. Against these criteria one has to conclude after all that the crisis will probably change little except to intensify existing negative tendencies.

Between philosophies

Behind the current tension on the secular left as to whether we should welcome the new 'wartime' solidarity engendered by the crisis, or rather bewail the inhibition of liberty that it brings in its wake, one can detect far older disagreements as to whether we are to think of the more alien face of the modern and the negatively dialectical impact of enlightenment in terms of primarily the Marxist alienation of labour on the one hand, or of Weberian bureaucratic control on the other—variously and sometimes alternatively seen as Heideggerean technocracy or as Foucauldian biopolitics. Is Capital the alienated human master agent which only the true agency of labour can overthrow, or is it rather the case that the problem is the very fantasising in practice of a single agency of control termed the 'State' which attempts to suppress the inherent multiplicity of agency through systems of complex intrusion into existential and vital levels of human reality? On this account, what we need to liberate is not unified human labour as the non-alienated human subjectivity, but a multiplicity of interacting agencies, both human and otherwise. Either human beings should suspend 'operation' and recover a mythical Edenic animality (Agamben) or else engage in a democratic constitutional negotiation with all other natural agents (Latour).

Depending on one's preference either for Marx or for 'the Weberian Left' one may see either promise or else menace in the current crisis. Yet one could argue that it is possible to synthesise these two perspectives on the negative aspect of the modern. On the one hand, labour is alienated in part because, as John Ruskin saw, materialism as such is unable to envisage a noble and spiritual end for work. On the other hand, the State does not just pursue power for its own sake, but also pursues an alienated power only defined as control because of the loss of a shared spiritual horizon. Just as capitalism needs to render naturally available goods scarce, and to invent new goods in short supply, if it is to sustain competition and profitability, so likewise our entire politics tends to 'economise' both life and other natural realities by rendering them selectively rare and more precarious, and by offering relatively exclusive remedies and 'solutions', subject at once to market forces and to bureaucratic regulation. In either case, power is increased to the same measure as profit, just as capitalist profit is inseparable from power.

What is sought, in either case, is the empty and narcissistic *libido dominandi*, as diagnosed by Saint Augustine. This is the aim of liberalism in the precise sense of a philosophy predicated on the primacy of the individual will. Ultimately, it is the failure of secular thought to isolate the shared framework of liberalism as the real problem that leads to the oscillation between alternatively money and power as the villain of modernity. Or else it is admitted that critique does *not* break with the liberal framework. Thus, inverting Viktor Orbán, Žižek roundly declares that 'Communists are liberals with a diploma'.[6] What this ultimately means for him is that the subject in her open freedom is dialectically identical with the open randomness of matter. Obviously this provides us with no metaphysical grounds upon which to question the operations of pure power, nor of alienated labour, nor of a seduction by illusory spectacle, nor yet of an ecological domination by human beings over nature, since this domination is, on this account, itself the most natural thing of all.

The equally metacritical and metaphysical task would rather be to discover not a dialectical identity between the subject and Nature, but a creative tension between them rooted in their shared participation in a transcendent order upholding the reality both of the spirit and of objectively desirable ends of spiritual expression through work upon matter and interaction with other natural agencies.

Between spiritualities

This brings me to the third tension, between those who celebrate our current concern with life as such and those who, in various degrees like Agamben, warn of our now being reduced to 'bare life', which will eventually prove to be no sort of life whatsoever. Interestingly, this debate has its ecclesiastical and theological equivalent: overwhelmingly, religious leaders have sanctified the new priority for the medical, but others have suggested that this is but an ultimate secular encouragement to see any old life as more important than a fulfilled spiritual one.[7] Thus they have argued against the shutting of churches and the ending of public worship.

Once again, both sides have a point. On the one hand, it is hysterical to claim that measures adopted in the face of war or plague are really intended in all perpetuity. And because we are embodied creatures, mere living is indeed the basis of more exalted modes of existence. On the other hand, we know very well that wartime emergency measures often do survive, though for good as well as for ill. It is also worryingly evident that churches have often been closed to an unnecessary degree and that they, along with other less utilitarian and more convivial public spaces (including libraries), are destined to be the last things to be re-opened, precisely because they are less about bare living and bare economic surviving.

In the longer term, just as we can see how the pandemic tends to increase human isolation and lack of real physical contact, thereby favouring a huge increase of 'divide and rule', so also we can see how it bodes to increase an over-obsession with the avoidance of danger and an endless and self-internalised quantification of risk from minute to minute. In the cases of motion and transport—of walking, climbing, cycling and sailing—as also with human, including sexual interactions, it is obvious that we do as individuals regard certain risks as constantly worth undergoing. We tend to become more inhibited by them when we look at averages and are provided with 'solutions' for their avoidance and minimisation. It is when we are persuaded to regard ourselves as objects through the gaze of the public spectacle that we cease to live with ourselves as self-posited subjects able spontaneously to sense which risks should be undergone and which avoided—all, of course according to inborn or acquired temperament, which is also part of 'who we are'.

The reverse side of this alienation from natural risk is the implicit taking on of a massive and generalised risk by combined Capital and power, which in reality exposes us all to exponentially increased risks of illness, both physical and mental, and ultimately of death, all of the time. So just as 'pure power' in fact depends, like Capital, upon rendering the natural scarce, so also an apparently sanitised removal of individual risk really depends upon an alienation of risk which consolidates it into one collective peril. Thus rule through the inhibition of risk is really rule through the permanent suspension (in both senses) of a huge axe over all of our heads.

We are only (as Agamben's work sees) reduced to 'bare life' because this life can ultimately be discarded, like the excluded scapegoat outside the gates of the city. For the logic of valuing life as such without risk is not that we *really* value life, but that all life has been economised—even and contradictorily the lives of the powerful and the rich themselves in the end. Liberalism is nihilism and inversion: if only negative freedom matters then this is only the disinhibition of material force and so it is identical with death. The churches should not then have gone so quiet during this crisis, nor have so readily colluded in rendering sacred spaces invisible.

The interruption of the interruption

If liberalism is ultimately the problem of a degenerate modernity and the lack of the excess of sacred indicators conserving the 'extra' of Spirit, then how are we to understand the release of locked-up energy with Black Lives Matter? However valid the cause (especially with regard to the utter scandal of US policing, juridical, prison, welfare and social services) a critical inquiry has to ask whether liberal opinion has turned to this in relief both from the unfathomable cultural/natural of the pandemic event and from its challenge to the hold of both economic liberalism and cultural hedonism. Here, supposedly, is a merely human and identifiable cause with supposedly clear and available solutions.

Therefore one can validly speculate that there has been a covert switch from one 'biological' topic to another more manageable one, just because it is only quasi-biological and so apparently more 'fixable'. Equally, the hyperbolic calls for sudden and immediate change in all our Western habits everywhere and with regard to everything would appear to parody the pandemic requirement for exceptional and manageable emergency. With the difference that *this* sovereign exception seems to be something not exercised over against us but rather by all of us. Once more, this diverts us from something problematically meta-human with which liberalism is complicit, to something more comfortably intra-human which liberalism can readily (it supposes) alter. It is not that racism is not a scourge: it obviously is; but there is an implicit and distracting danger of momentarily thinking that it is *the* scourge. Indeed, an inflated 'anti-racism' seems to proffer itself as the newly sacral iconoclastic counter-religion, the ultimate Protestantism of the West refusing the West as an ancient mouldering idol from start to finish.

Between nature and humanity

How might our current situation and the above reflections relate to our wider current and future ecological crisis? Many have noted how nature seems to flourish more without us: birds sing louder, fish return to canals, deer wander more freely and right into the heart of our towns. Others, however, have pointed out how this is in part misleading. Red kites miss road-kill, and many more domesticated animals and plants languish outside our tending. It is not actually ecological to think in terms of humans over against a single unified natural world: no, we are one of many natural agents and as natural we have a good (even perhaps biblical and superintending) natural role to play. The point is not the liberal alternative of either dominating or liberating nature, but the communitarian one of getting the right balance between different natural actors and between an open human subjectivity and relatively more fixed natural agencies. They need our free and adaptable nurture; we need their stimulus and content if we are to fulfil ourselves.

To think in terms of a need of surrender to a supposedly fixed and perfectly unified natural order is both dangerous and actually unecological, as Timothy Morton has argued.[8] For it would be rule by global experts claiming to determine the ecological optimum in terms of maximal sustainability. But it is unecological to imagine that such a calculation is ever possible. Since natural connections are infinitely ramifying, and since nature can be spontaneous and unpredictable, all we ever have to go on are good guesses and situated, well-attuned local hunches and intuitions.

Ecology is also *not* committed to the idea that the resources of the planet are naturally finite without our intervention: to the contrary, just because they are temporal and self-renewing they are serially infinite. As with the capitalist and State exploitation of human life, so also with the exploitation of life in general—scarcity is something *humanly produced* in order to stimulate competitive demand and increased profit and to tighten centralised control.

It might seem that this refusal of a puritanical mode of ecologism is untheological. Yet if we follow Eriugena and Cusanus (building upon Augustine) in seeing that creatures precisely as being created only from nothing are participatively self-creators (since there is nothing 'beneath' their reception of the divine creative act, which simply *is* what they are), then we will see that theology does not need to endorse any false notion of a fixed 'nature' which extrinsically disciplines us, even while insisting on the recognition of emergent 'true essences' or characters. The best theology has always known that the created universe is rather one of multiple actors in shifting relationships, and that the world is only a unity at all through the divine grounding which infinitely exceeds it. At the same time, theology endorses an unabashed anthropocentricity, because it understands that human creative action reaches furthest, both for ill and for good, though never in fantasised independence of other creatures. That fantasied independent action, which is *merely* technological, is actually not really creative at all.

Theology can better understand all this in terms of the participation of human creativity not just in the externally creative divine action, but also in the supremely dynamic and yet supremely restful life of the Trinity.[9] For God the Father and origin does not contain a 'fixed plan' to which the Son and the Spirit are subservient. Instead, the Father's reasoning is nothing other than his full realised expression in the *Ars* which is his Son, as both Bonaventure and Aquinas put it, and the Father's initiating life is nothing other than the Spirit's interpretative reception of and response to this art. For Eriugena's terminology this is the completion of the filial active *virtus* by the spiritual *operatio* or fully completed act.[10] This third and binding moment shows how, as it were, the Paternal expression in the Son is both infinitely complete and yet mysteriously not complete after all. It is always the further existential response to the expression which accompanies the very origin that alone completes Being as both personal and 'characterised'.

Thus the radicalism of the doctrine of the Trinity consists in the fact that it does not take even the Absolute as negating or cancelling the created processes of groping towards the ends of labour, nor the endless readings of the products of labour which constitute community as reception of and circulation of gift, but rather regards it as realising all this eternally and infinitely. It follows that we do not share in and echo God according to our fixed notions, nor our theoretical surmises, but by our feeling, hoping and striving, and by our re-considering and re-relating.

Is a doctrine of participation in Creation and in the Trinity just a superfluous icing on the cake of ecological thought? One can argue that it is much more than that. For secular thought still tends to veer between a perspectival anthropomorphism after Kant—perhaps generalised, as by Graham Harman and Morton in his wake, to all existing entities—and a sheer naturalism which would deny any human, or even any animal or chemical uniqueness.

This is because metaphysical immanentism needs to produce an immanent absolute in place of God—either Man or Nature. Bruno Latour certainly sees this, but only with ambivalence does he suggest that we therefore cannot remain in pure immanence.[11] Indeed, at the political level he wants a kind of constitutional democracy to arise between the scientistic proponents of immanence and the religious proponents of transcendence. But wherein could any such compromise possibly lie? It would only be a liberal formalism once more, not the sort of thick, relational open-ended global network of integral places without any single centre of sovereignty that Latour so rightly desires.

Instead, theology must boldly say that secular thought typically cannot resolve and often pretends to evade the ontological *aporias* of relationality versus integral thing, of process versus substance, of part versus whole, of logic versus invention and of unique human spirit versus natural solidarity. Beyond immanence, the invocation of transcendence allows these pairs to remain in unresolved play and in ecological balance. Within immanence we are teasingly shuttled between all these poles, because all of them are mere totem-shadows, only real as reflecting the light of God, which, however, they themselves creatively ignite and beam forth. They *are* this self-ignition and conveyed further radiance. And the fully conscious self-ignitings and out-beamings which are human persons both lie entirely within space and time and yet are able to transcend it. A better ecology would allow *at once* that human beings are enclosed within the world *and* that they can exceed it, that the duality of the globe as both real container and surveyable round map is not wrong, if nonetheless aporetic. It is by virtue of their metaphysically cosmonautical survey of the globe from an imagined afar that humans are indeed able to be its stewards and gardeners after

Adam and rightly to name the beasts (which means after Dionysius receiving their theophanic disclosures) not dominate them.

For the God of Christianity is not a super-totality: he is beyond universality and individuality, and as Trinitarian lies also beyond the contrast of substance and relation, unity and plurality, process and thing, nature and person. For theology indeed, the *event* as a mysterious and unfathomable synthesis of the personal and the natural can be in disclosive excess of the totality, without this signalling an immanentist anarchy. For the event, whether positive or negative, or both, as *revelatory*, can point beyond immanent closure to an infinite transcendence in excess of even any possible totality, just as the Gospel of John ends by saying that the story of the event of Christ is bigger than the entire world.

In particular, we encounter the strange coincidence of person with essence, or subject with 'predicated' character, not just in surprising events, both public and private, but in every 'sudden' moment (as Plato taught in the *Parmenides*) that composes our lives in terms of the 'present' synthesis of selective memory and imaginative anticipation.[12] In part we seem to elect natural things and past human things, and in part they seem to 'adopt' us. In this way the non-existent pure interval of the subjective 'moment' or 'now' seems to mediate to us eternity in terms of such an ineffable balance between open freedom and arriving, characterising content.

One can suggest that this experienced coincidence of essence with subjectivity grounds the more ultimate equality of all created things with human beings. For even though humans are within immanence the supreme creators and guardians, they are only so if they fully respect their complex situatedness, and vulnerability to influence, under the equal creative supremacy of *Gaia* taken as a real, albeit elusive whole which is the world-soul, or God in his sophianic, immanent presence, as both Plato and the Bible teach us.

We need this philosophical and theological vision and to act on it, if we are to save our planet from ourselves and ourselves along with our planet. In order to do so, we must deny neither our higher human personhood, nor our immersion in nature, which in another sense exceeds us. We have to admit the superiority of person in one respect and of essence in another—as within the divine Trinity from whom the Creation pours forth. In order to rescue other creatures alongside ourselves, we need to act paradoxically as their kenotic saviours—at once as architectonic coordinators and yet also in humble partnership with them and in tune with the Created wisdom of God that mysteriously holds all of Creation together.

The same Trinitarian model holds good at an intra-human level. A good relationship to nature requires us to get into more immediate personal contact with our local environment which needs to be more self-governing and self-sufficient in both ecological and political terms. At the same time, we cannot ignore our essential, humanly specific and planetary unity which requires far better international coordination if we are to survive, let alone flourish. This should not be thought of in terms some sort of implausible world government, directed by personal rulers. Yet global coordination is all the same required, and this cannot be just 'impersonal', or a matter of fixed rules and procedures, if it is to work. There seems to be something here in terms of shared sovereignty and mutual international self-government that is still to be invented. But for certain this requires an emergent sense of a global metaphysical culture, a sense of shared global sacrality that alone can secure the place of Spirit and so the dignity of human labour and of all other natural agencies.

Notes

1. Alain Badiou, 'On the Epidemic Situation' in *Verso*, online at https://www.versobooks.com.
2. Bruno Latour, 'Is This a Dress Rehearsal' in *critinq*, online at https://critinq.wordpress.com.
3. Bruno Latour, 'Le surplus de subsistance' in *Esprit*, May, 2020 online at http://esprit.presse.fr.
4. Slavoj Žižek, *Pandemic! Covid 19 Shakes the World* (Cambridge: Polity, 2020).
5. Giorgio Agamben, 'The Invention of an Epidemic' in *European Journal of Psychoanalysis* online at https://www.journal-psychoanalysis.eu.
6. Žižek, *Pandemic*, 46.
7. R.R. Reno, 'Coronavirus Reality Check' in *First Things*, April 27th, 2020, online at https://www.firstthings.com.
8. Timothy Morton, *Being Ecological* (London: Penguin, 2018).
9. Pope Francis, *Praise Be to You: Laudato Si: On Care for Our Common Home* (San Francisco: Ignatius, 2015).
10. For example, John Scottus Eriugena, *Periphyseon*, Book I, 507B 10–15.
11. Bruno Latour, *Facing Gaia: Eight Lectures on the New Climactic Regime* (Cambridge: Polity, 2017).
12. See Sergij Bulgakov, *The Tragedy of Philosophy*, trans. Stephen Churchyard, with a preface by John Milbank (New York: Angelico, 2020).

8 COVID-19, human ecology and the ontological turn to Gaia

Michael Northcott

Introduction

The COVID-19 crisis is at one and the same time a public health crisis and a social crisis of momentous proportions. The exceptional impacts of the crisis are not connected with actual fatality from the virus, which at less than one million globally is no higher than seasonal flu and only a small fraction of mortality in historic pandemics such as the 'Spanish flu' which killed over 50 million in a world population one quarter of the present, but rather with the effects of the large-scale social isolation of individuals and households, the shuttering of huge numbers of small businesses, subsistence farms, and most workplaces over an extended period, and the global roll-out of states of emergency and suspensions of normal human freedoms and behaviours such as family and religious gatherings, cultural and educational activities, travel and so on. Never before in history has humanity quarantined the healthy in response to a disease outbreak. There was therefore no evidential basis for the policy although there was extensive prior evidence concerning increased mortality from the predictable global economic depression, large-scale hunger, and mental health crisis, that it caused. Although the quarantining was said to protect those particularly at risk of mortality from SARS-CoV2, over 80% of excess mortality in the peak month of April in Europe and North America was of elderly care home residents with existing serious health conditions, precisely those in whose name the measures were taken.

To call the crisis a 'natural disaster' or even a 'natural evil' would therefore be misleading. This is further underwritten by the fact that the novel SARS-CoV2 virus originated in risky human practices and not in natural events, and in particular the isolation, and 'gain of function' manipulation of a horsehoe bat virus from a cave in Yunan in the laboratory of the University of North Carolina and the Wuhan virology laboratory, results of which are reported in peer reviewed papers by scientists from both laboratories.[1] The peculiarly humanly adapted nature of the SARS-CoV2 virus, and the features it shares with the gain of function virus reported on in *Nature Medicine* in 2015, indicate it is highly likely the chimeric virus was accidentally released from the Wuhan laboratory.[2] This is underscored by the fact that the earliest victims of the virus had no association with the Wuhan wet market, that live bats are not sold in the market, and that the genetic profiles of the virus isolated from victims associated with the Wuhan wet market had a 100% match to the SARS-CoV2 virus and are not therefore evidence of zoonotic development and transmission from nonhumans to humans prior to human infection.[3]

In the light of the role of human encroachments on wild habitats where the precursor to the chimeric virus was captured, and the subsequent laboratory production of versions of the virus capable of infecting mammals, it is clear that the theological implications of the present crisis are better envisaged not in terms of theodicy, as for example Albert Camus' *La Peste* written after the Spanish flu, but as a heightening of the existing ecological and technological crisis in which the human re-engineering of ecosystems and habitats across the whole Earth's surface generates a growing threat of extinction for huge numbers of nonhuman species, and growing risks to the health and safety of humans. The crisis therefore heightens the onto-theological question of the status of the divine creation prior to its modification and re-engineering by humans.

Viral states of emergency, the climate regime and 'One Health'

The social response to the emergence of SARS-CoV2 represents a top-down Statist project coordinated by the World Health Organisation, Centres for Disease Control in North America, Europe and Asia, and central banks who globally created unprecedented quantities of digital money to support large corporations and stock markets, and to a lesser extent aid the billions of individuals and entrepreneurs who lost income—in many cases to the point of hunger, penury and even suicide—during the unprecedented economic shutdown.[4] The SARS-CoV2 regime did not however shutter the activities of large corporations and indeed represented a huge economic bonanza for giant tech corporations such as Amazon, Alphabet, Apple, Facebook and Tesla, while it also tilted the economic balance towards large-scale retailers—and particularly supermarkets—which were permitted to stay open while traditional markets, delicatessens, bakers, farmers markets and other small businesses were all forcibly closed for many months.[5]

This significant shift of economic activity from informal actors and small businesses to giant corporations is reminiscent of the global climate regime enacted by the United Nations Framework Convention on Climate Change which has for over 20 years focused efforts to address climate change on top-down solutions, and in particular national carbon accounts and 'carbon trading', as favoured by nation states, investors and energy corporations.[6] These 'solutions' have notably failed to stop states and corporations from extracting and marketing fossil fuels, or from destroying the capacity of ecosystems to absorb the resultant greenhouse gas emissions because of ongoing destruction of significant carbon sinks such as tropical forests on land, and kelp and mangrove forests and other critical features of the huge 'carbon pump' of the marine environment. The top-down corporately shaped climate regime is analogous to the response to SARS-CoV2 because it suggests that only government and intergovernmental agencies acting in concert with large technologically sophisticated global corporations are capable of securing the welfare of people and planet in a global emergency such as the virus is said to represent.

Against top-down globalist solutions to the ecological crisis, environmental history suggests that effective resistance to the forces driving the ecological crisis did not come in the first instance from scientists, governments or corporations but rather from groups of citizens acting together in defence of particular places and species which they saw as being threatened by the pace and destructive power of industrial technologies. Pioneering efforts in the first centuries of the industrial revolution to protect what were seen as precious landscapes—such as the English Lake District or the Californian Sierra—from destruction originated in protest campaigns against industrial infrastructure, and atmospheric pollution, by artists, priests and poets such as John Ruskin, Canon Hardwick Rawnsley, William Wordsworth and John Muir. These bottom-up efforts generated popular cultural shifts in human appreciation of the nonhuman which in turn led to efforts to open up access to wilderness areas for human recreation as well as to protect them from economic desecration.[7] But despite the bottom-up origins of modern environmentalism, these pioneering efforts were eventually captured by state actors who created protected areas and National Parks of the kind that now cover 2% of the earth's land area. And the same states which designate and protect National and State Parks also license and subsidise farming, fishing, forestry and mining corporations as they encroach on the last remnants of old growth forest, and other precious unmodified ecosystems, in the continuing extractive turn of the global economy towards the nonhuman earth.[8] In Brazil and Indonesia there is already evidence that, far from reducing economically driven destruction of tropical forests, the SARS-CoV2 crisis occasioned increased licence for forest burning and conversion to monocultures in areas such as the Amazon, Borneo and Sumatra.[9]

The conversion of the nonhuman world outside the 2% proportion of the earth that is protected into industrial extractive and farming zones is pushing the trajectory of the Earth and her ecosystems from the state of maximal species diversity that evolved over 3.5 billion years, and which accompanied the evolution of *Homo sapiens*, to one of significantly reduced biodiversity in which the dominant species of animal and plant on the planet are domesticated by humans and suited for large-scale industrial food production systems. Just five plants and four animals are now responsible for the majority of human calorific intake, and this corporately dominated, and increasingly monocultural food system is having detrimental impacts on the diversity and health of soils, water catchments and the marine environment as well as forests and grasslands. It is also detrimentally impacting human health.

Analogous to the state and corporate dominance of the climate and environmental regimes, the World Health Organisation along with the Gates Foundation and the World Economic Forum is promoting a top-down agenda for global health, often associated with the 'One Health' project to combine medical and veterinary science.[10] One vision for global health monitoring that has been promoted by the viral emergency is a global health and vaccination database accessible to governments and other agencies at borders and other sensitive locations.[11] The top-down One Health agenda is receiving a considerable fillip from the SARS-CoV2 states of emergency as governments contributed 7.5 billion dollars in a London webinar hosted by the British government to the Global Alliance for Vaccination on 4 June 2020 in support of an unprecedented proposal to vaccinate the global population against the disease caused by SARS-CoV2, although no successful vaccine has ever been developed for more than 200 coronaviruses already in circulation in the human population.[12]

Against the One Health agenda, there has for the last 30 years been growing attention by gastroenterologists, nutritionists and complementary therapists to the human biome as the core of an individual's health and immune system. 'Biome' therapy favours a diet that is high in unprocessed plant diversity, and low in industrially favoured staples including refined carbohydrates, refined fats, sugar, meat and dairy products. Such a diet supports the health and functioning of one to two trillion bacteria and viruses that constitute and sustain a healthy body and strong immune system in its relations with other bodies and the environment, and in its ability to resist and expel pathogens and toxins including the SARS-CoV2 virus.[13] Such a diet also improves mental state as well as supporting optimal functioning of internal organs and the body as a whole and reducing mortality from cancers, heart disease and strokes.[14] But such a diet is inconsistent with the top-down corporately controlled monocultural production of meats, fats, sugars and cereals, and their conversion into highly processed foods, and the long-distance centralised supply chains, favoured by food corporations and supermarkets. It is also inconsistent with the One Health agenda which views human immunity not as a function of an individual's diet, and of their internal microbial ecosystem, but as a function of big pharmaceutical companies, vaccination programmes and global disease control strategies. The chasm between a top-down approach and a bottom-up approach here too demonstrates the already existing ecological and socio-political crisis, and the pandemic's heightening of that crisis.

The historic and religious roots of human ecology

It is widely believed that 'environmental regulation' began with the creation of state agencies such as the United States Environmental Protection Agency in 1970. But environmental regulation is a process that developed over thousands of years as groups of individuals began to work together to create habitats and environments in which they grew and irrigated crops and domesticated animals through a range of different kinds of collective action.

The oldest records of bottom-up rules and regulations about the uses of other kind in human food and service provision are to be found in religious texts such as the Vedas and the Hebrew Bible, and are often preserved in ritual customs—such as dietary laws—whose original ecosystem, human health and hygiene functions are long forgotten. Mary Douglas argues that rules about diet, irrigation and protection of certain places and practices—and especially the riskier practices of raising and slaughtering animals—in the Hebrew Bible have ecological and human health functions, although these were generally dismissed by the originators of the scientific study of religion as 'magic' or 'superstition', so confining the scientific study of the meanings and purposes of religions to their ethical functions.[15] In a similar vein to Douglas, Roy Rappaport pioneered the study of the ecological function of indigenous religion when he investigated the pig keeping and sacrificial customs of a tribe in Papua New Guinea and found that their religious practices enabled them to keep their numbers of domesticated animals within the carrying capacity of their ecosystem habitat.[16] Alongside the anthropological discovery of the ecological function of religion and religious communities, historians have traced the genealogical roots of Alpine pastoral governance systems, to the communitarian and religious character of Alpine villages in the Middle Ages.[17] Anthropological and historical investigations of non-State and non-Corporate environmental governance have evolved into a larger field of investigation of commons governance procedures in pre-industrial and non-State societies pioneered by Elinor Ostrom.[18]

There are also analogies between the communitarian and religious origins of environmental regulation and contemporary efforts by indigenous peoples to resist encroachments by State-licensed corporate actors into the last relatively intact ecosystems in the Amazon, in Central Africa and in Southeast Asia, and which Juan Martinez-Alier calls the 'environmentalism of the poor'.[19] This contemporary bottom-up environmentalism represents the efforts of indigenous people to preserve not only their livelihoods and ancestral habitats, but also their agency as intergenerational ecosystem guardians. As Pope Francis notes in *Laudato Si'* indigenous people have been the most effective guardians of ecosystems globally over thousands of years but they face at the present time unprecedented encroachments on their habitats, including violence directed to community organisers who attempt to resist these.[20]

These developments in the study of human ecology indicate that relationships between people and their habitats of the kind which sustain the biodiversity and hence resilience of ecosystems, while also sustaining the health and immune strength of persons, are 'polycentric'. Such relationships are not characterised by the two dominant institutions in modern agriculture and food provision, and in public health, which is to say large economic corporations, and state agencies. Instead they are characterised by a range of taboos, traditions, social agreements, rules, institutions and customs which evolved over time in diverse ways as suited the diverse ecological conditions of different human ecological habitats, and which originated and in many cases are still sustained by religiously underwritten communitarianism.

The ontological turn to Gaia and the doctrine of creation

The attempted monopolisation by a small number of intergovernmental agencies and corporations of human health, habitat and nutrition is indicative of a globalist culture in which agency is taken from the many—both human and nonhuman—by the few: David Graeber dubbed them the 'one per cent', though it would be more accurate to call them the 0.1%.[21]

Against this way of thinking and acting, anthropologists and philosophers have inaugurated what they call an 'ontological turn' arising from attention to and description of the ways in which indigenous cultures honour and partner with the agency of nonhuman 'others', including ecosystems, plants and animals in the co-assembly and co-sustaining of their communities, cultures, customs and habitats and in the provision of food, shelter and the other core elements of human life.[22] The ontological turn involves rejection of the standard post-Cartesian dualisms of mentality and physicality, nature and culture, persons and things, persons and species, and recalls instead premodern metaphysical realism in which thoughts about objects are said to be not just resident in minds but co-constructed by object-mind encounters and hence by things in their actuality.[23] The theological basis for metaphysical realism is that the human mind is 'creation-shaped', and hence mental objects are 'real' analogies with the material and organic beings which they represent, and not merely apprehensions. This approach challenges the Humean fact-value distinction and, as deep ecologists such as Arne Naess and Warwick Fox argue, provides a 'way back' from the modern philosophical dismissal of the agency of the nonhuman in constructing what humans call 'valuable' in their earthly habitat including biodiversity, climate stability and ecosystem resilience.[24] The ontological turn is also prominent in Bruno Latour's *oeuvre* on how to think, and how to do politics and science, in the planetary emergency of climate change and the Anthropocene.[25]

There is however a notable lack of attention to the ontological turn in Christian theology which is surprising since, as I first suggested in 1996, there is a remarkable accord between metaphysical realism of the kind suggested by deep ecologists such as Naess and Fox, who anticipated the ontological turn, and the metaphysical realism of the medieval Christian synthesis of Thomas Aquinas.[26] Critics of attempts to revive metaphysical realism argue that it neglects the rationale for the Enlightenment fact-value distinction which was occasioned by the rise of Newtonian science which demonstrated a fundamental non-correspondence between human apprehensions of the material world—such as the appearance that the sun is rising and falling in the sky—and the actual material constitution and functioning of heavenly and earthly bodies. This non-correspondence between mentality and cosmos therefore required the innovation of the Humean fact-value distinction, and the related Kantian epistemological innovation of two forms of rationality, and a political constitution which split apart nature and culture, organisms and thoughts. To answer this criticism it is only necessary to note that the relatively static cosmology suggested by Newtonianism has now given way to a new cosmological paradigm under the twin influences of earth system science and quantum mechanics, and that in this new paradigm correspondence between mentality and things in themselves finds a scientific as well as a philosophical foundation.

What is now called 'earth system science' has its recent origin in the Gaia theory of James Lovelock. The Gaia theory involves the claim that all the beings resident in the 'critical zone' that stretches from subterranean and submarine hot rocks to the upper atmosphere 30 kilometres above the Earth's surface express agency individually and collectively in generating and sustaining a planetary atmosphere, climatic conditions, chemical composition and organic processes which make life, including human life, possible.[27] While James Hutton, the 'father' of modern geology and of deep time, anticipated aspects of the Gaia theory in his eighteenth-century account of the Theory of the Earth as a system in which volcanoes, forests, soils and oceans all interact to create mediums for plants and animals to evolve, Lovelock's theory added a crucial new element which is that the proportions of gases in the atmosphere suitable for the evolution of forests and then for oxygen-breathing mammals are a function of the agency of life in all its forms, from lichen on, and weathering of, rocks to phytoplankton in the oceans and microbiota in submarine trenches. No modern scientist before Lovelock had envisaged planetary sustaining agency stretching that extensively across every kind of life form in what medieval theologians once called the 'great chain of being'.

The Gaia theory, which is now widely accepted by mainstream scientists, is analogous to Aristotle's divinity-centred cosmos, and to Plato's theological account of creation in the *Timaeus*. It also finds analogy with Hindu beliefs in the Trinitarian structure of Brahma, Vishnu and Shiva according to which all beings are continuously flowing in the karmic cycle of being and nonbeing from Brahma (the Creator) through Vishnu (the Sustainer) to Shiva (the Eliminator/Recycler). But such analogies are not so evident in relation to the Abrahamic faiths which are resistant to the idea of the earth as a living entity. This is in large part because what has become known as the 'mainstream' Abrahamic account of being and creation—i.e. the account of this idea which has attracted majority opinion in Judaism, Christianity and Islam—posits a divine Creator who, from a spatially and temporally extra-terrestrial order of divine being, generates the universe, earth and living beings on the earth *ex nihilo* or out of nothing. Some versions of creationism also hold, as all pre-Darwinian creationists did, that each individual species, and the current state of the earth, including its material forms of mountains, rivers, plains, lakes and oceans and its balance of gases, were originally generated or 'authored' as they now appear by the Creator, thus denying a core tenet of evolutionary science which is change over Deep Time.

The 'way back' in Christian theology from an anti-scientific early modern creationism, and a related static natural theology, to a more fluid and interpenetrative relationship between the divine agency and the agency of living beings in creating all that is, was first suggested by Friedrich Schleiermacher's valuable but under-utilised account of divine creative activity as continuous. Schleiermacher well understood that the early modern development of the doctrine of divine providence as a way to explain the sustaining work of the Spirit in creation while preserving the idea of an original and definitive First Cause type of ordering of creation was a problematic development which neither satisfactorily responded to modern discoveries of the extent of change that the earth has undergone over its long geohistory, nor preserved the idea of a divine creator in a manner consistent with that geohistory. He proposed the solution in *The Christian Faith* as follows:

> The divine causality as equivalent in compass to the sum-total of the natural order is expressed in the term, the divine omnipotence; this puts the whole of finite being under the divine causality. The divine causality as opposed to the finite and natural is expressed in the term, the divine eternity. That is, the interrelationship of partial causality and passivity makes the natural order a sphere of reciprocal action, and thus of change as such, in that all change and all alteration can be traced back to this antithesis. It is therefore just in the relationship in which the natural causality is set over against the divine, that the essence of the former is to be temporal; and consequently, so far as eternal is the opposite of temporal, the eternity of God will also be the expression of that antithesis.[28]

Schleiermacher in this dense passage suggests that the traditional idea of 'First Cause' is misleading and that the doctrine of creation is more consistent with modern conceptions of an evolving and changing set of processes when causation is envisaged as a continuing divine characteristic of the natural order rather than a single temporal event or set of events and that this approach 'makes the natural order a sphere of reciprocal action'. This neat solution does indeed sound Gaian, and it unfolds elsewhere in the *Christian Faith* into the idea that not only the natural order but the Christological incarnation of the divine is also a continuing rather than a once for all event when it is experienced by individuals in the feeling of dependence on the divine, and in which the Incarnation becomes known in its actuality by those who are 'in Christ'.[29]

There is a vast literature on the question of divine agency in earthly processes and relations, but in essence Schleiermacher's solution is to refuse that there is a contest between divinity and earthly life in the agency of the processes of change and relation which co-assemble a habitable world, as the Gaia theory proposes, because to the extent that these processes are causative they *participate* in the original divine causation of all things while at the same time expressing the agency of creaturely beings. There is no divine 'crowding out' of multiple agencies on this approach but rather agency has a divine and an earthly aspect. Schleiermacher's solution is in accord with the most recent findings in particle physics, as well as in the human biome: agency goes all the way down, even to microbes in human stomachs and the tiniest atomic particles whose agency always carries an element of indeterminacy, or openness, within it, as Alfred North Whitehead argued in *Process and Reality*, and as Walter Heisenberg demonstrated in the laboratory.

A viral conclusion

The idea of agency expressed in every atom and microbe as *participation* in divine creativity does not immediately suggest easy resolutions of the ecological crisis and the overwhelming, by the scale and global spread of human industrial activities, of the agency of other creatures and the influence of assemblies of creatures on ecosystems and more broadly the Earth system or Gaia. But it does suggest a stronger theological basis for recovering respect for the given order of species and ecosystems, and their divinely given agency in sustaining a habitable earth, than other formulations of the doctrine of creation in modern theology, and not least the timeless and static account of creation offered in Karl Barth's influential *Church Dogmatics*.

The current emergency has conferred enormous agency on an invisible virus which is so small that it can easily pass through the fetishised non-medical masks that many people spontaneously adopted, and which many governments mandated, supposedly to ward it off despite complete lack of medical evidence of their effectiveness. While the current crisis may not be a natural disaster, given the origins of the virus in unwise human practices in mixing genes and species that in the wild are not found together, it nonetheless has revealed the enduring potential of the indeterminate agency of the nonhuman to profoundly influence, for good or ill, science-informed and technologically empowered humans.

On the top-down response to the crisis, and the broader political and economic tendencies of surveillance and control that it portends, the Gaian and theological vision of earth and earthly beings, as reciprocally agential from the ocean's depths to the heights of heaven, is a source of inspiration for an alternative vision in which the co-creation of the health and habitat of people and of nonhuman beings are not subjected to monopolistic control by a small number of human actors, for many of whom profit remains the aim and not health, either human or planetary. Doctrine is never enough without action, but thinking critically and genealogically in the midst of a global media management exercise of an unprecedentedly coordinated kind has never been more needed to inform resistance that is genealogically wise and not merely reactive or even hysterical.

Notes

1 Vineet D Menachery, Boyd L Yount Jr, Kari Debbink et al, 'A SARS-like cluster of circulating bat coronaviruses shows potential for human emergence', *Nature Medicine* 21 (2015) 1508–14
2 Ben Hul, Lei-Ping Zengl, Xing-Lou Yang et al, 'Discovery of a rich gene pool of bat SARS- related coronaviruses provides new insights into the origin of SARS coronavirus', *PLoS Pathog* 13(11): e1006698. https://doi.org/10.1371/ journal.ppat.1006698
3 Shing Hei Zhan, Benjamin E. Deverman, Yujia Alina Chan et al, 'SARS-CoV-2 is well adapted for humans. What does this mean for re-emergence?', *bioRxiv* (May 2020) https://doi.org/10.1101/2020.05.01.073262.
4 Andrew M. Miller, 'California doctors say they've seen more deaths from suicide than coronavirus since lockdown', *Washington Post*, May 21, 2020, https://www.washingtonexaminer.com/news/california-doctors-say-theyve-seen-more-deaths-from-suicide-than-coronavirus-since-lockdowns, accessed June 25, 2020.
5 Omar Hassan, 'Coronavirus will bankrupt more people than it kills—and that's the real global emergency', *The Independent*, March 11, 2020, https://www.independent.co.uk/voices/coronavirus-deaths-trump-stock-market-pandemic-economy-bankrupt-italy-a9394891.html, accessed June 25, 2020.
6 See Michael S. Northcott, *A Moral Climate: The Ethics of Global Warming* (London: Darton Longman and Todd, 2007) and *A Political Theology of Climate Change* (Grand Rapids, MI: Wm. B. Eerdmans, 2013).
7 See Michael S. Northcott, 'The romantics, the English Lake District, and the sacredness of high land: mountains as hierophanic places in the

origins of environmentalism and nature conservation', in Martin Illert and Gunter Heimbrock, eds., *Ecotheology. Essays in Honour of Sigurd Bergmann* (Frankfurt: Brill, forthcoming).
8 See Kyle Vanhoutan and Michael S. Northcott, 'Nature and the nation-state: ambivalence, evil and American environmentalism', in Kyle Vanhoutan and Michael S. Northcott, eds., *Diversity and Dominion: Dialogues in Ecology, Ethics, and Theology* (Eugene, ON: Cascade Books, 2009), 138–156.
9 Henry Holloway, 'Cash from Chaos: Amazon rainforest 'being destroyed at a record rate in coronavirus lockdown as illegal loggers exploit crisis'', *The Sun*, April 22, 2020, https://www.thesun.co.uk/news/11457140/amazon-rainforest-deforestation-coronavirus-lockdown-illegal-loggers/ accessed June 25, 2020.
10 Bruce Kaplan and Mary Echols, 'One Health' – the Rosetta stone for 21st century health and health providers', *Veterinaria Italiana*, 45 (2009), 377–382.
11 See https://www.digitalindia.gov.in/infrastructure, accessed June 23, 2020: for a critical perspective see Shyam Divan, 'The Prime Minister's fingerprints: Aadhar and the garrotting of civil liberties', *National Law School of India Review*, 26 (2014), 159–168.
12 Global Vaccine Summit 2020 London: Chair's Summary, https://www.gavi.org/sites/default/files/2020-06/4-June-2020-Global-Vaccine-Summit-Gavi-3rd-Replenishment-Chairs-Summary.pdf, accessed 25 June, 2020.
13 Mark L. Heiman and Frank L. Greenway, 'A healthy gastrointestinal microbiome is dependent on dietary diversity', *Molecular Metabolism*, 5 (2016), 317–320.
14 See Susan L. Prescott and Alan C. Logan, *The Secret Life of Your Microbiome: Why Nature and Biodiversity Are Essential to Health and Happiness* (Gabriola Island: New Society Publ., 2017); Javier Cabrera-Perez, Vladimir P. Badinovac and Thomas S. Griffith, 'Enteric immunity, the gut microbiome, and sepsis: rethinking the germ theory of disease', *Experimental Biology and Medicine*, 242 (2017), 127–139; Clair R. Martin, Vadim Osadchiy, Amir Kalani et al., 'The brain-gut microbiome axis', *Cellular and Molecular Gastroenterology and Hepatology*, 6 (2018), 133–148.
15 Mary Douglas, *Purity and Danger: An Analysis of the Concepts of Pollution and Taboo* (London: Routledge, 1966), 32–39.
16 Roy A. Rappaport, *Pigs for the Ancestors: Ritual in the Ecology of a New Guinea People* (New Haven, CT: Yale University Press, 1969).
17 Robert McC. Netting, 'The system nobody know: village irrigation in the Swiss Alps', in McG. Gibson and Thomas E. Downing, eds., *The Impact of Irrigation in Society* (Tucson: University of Arizona Press, 1977), 67–75.
18 Elinor Ostrom, *Governing the Commons: The Evolution of Institutions for Collective Action* (Cambridge: Cambridge University Press, 1990): on the pre-modern history of environmental governance see further Sean Coyle and Karen Morrow, *The Philosophical Foundations of Environmental Law: Property, Rights and Nature* (Oxford: Hart Publ. 2005).
19 Juan Martinez-Alier, *The Environmentalism of the Poor: A Study of Ecological Conflicts and Valuation* (Cheltenham: Edward Elgar, 2003).
20 *Encyclical Letter Laudato Si' of the Holy Father Francis on Care for Our Common Home* (Vatican City: Libreria Editrice Vaticana, 2015), 146.

21 David Graeber, *The Democracy Project: A History, a Crisis, a Movement* (New York: Spiegel and Grau, 2013), 115–12; on the neo-imperial dimensions of the 'global public health' project see Jacob Levich, '*The Gates Foundation, Ebola, and Global Health Imperialism*', *American Journal of Economics and Sociology*, 74, (2015) 704–742.
22 In addition to Rappaport, *Pigs for the Ancestors* see his *Ecology, Meaning and Religion* (Richmond, CA: Atlantic Books, 1979), see also Donna Haraway, *Primate Visions: Gender, Race, and Nature in the World of Modern Science* (New York: Routledge, 1989), and Donna Haraway, *Staying with the Trouble: Making Kin in the Chthulucene* (Durham, NC: Duke University Press, 2015); Philippe Descola, *Beyond Nature and Culture*, trans. Janet Lloyd, foreword by Marshall Sahlins (Chicago, IL: University of Chicago Press, 2013).
23 For an overview of the metaphysical implications of the ontological turn for modern philosophy see John Heil, *The Universe As We Find It* (Oxford: Oxford University Press, 2012): arguably Martin Heidegger was the first modern philosopher to anticipate the ontological turn in Martin Heidegger, *What Is a Thing?* trans. W.B. Barton and Vera Deutsch with an analysis by Eugene T. Gendlin (Chicago, IL: H. Regnery and Co., 1970).
24 See Arne Naess with Per Ingvar Haukelan, *Life's Philosophy: Reason & Feeling in a Deeper World*, trans. Roland Huntford with a foreword by Bill McKibben and an introduction by Harold Glasser (Athens: University of Georgia Press, 2002); Warwick Fox, *Toward a Transpersonal Ecology: Developing New Foundations for Environmentalism* (Dartington: Green Books, 1995).
25 Bruno Latour, *The Politics of Nature: How to Bring the Sciences into Democracy*, trans. Catherine Porter (Cambridge, MA: Harvard University Press, 2004).
26 Michael S. Northcott, *The Environment and Christian Ethics* (Cambridge: Cambridge University Press, 1996): see also Michael S. Northcott, 'Do Dolphins Carry the Cross? Biological Moral Realism and Theological Ethics', *New Blackfriars*, 84 (2003), 540–553.
27 James Lovelock, *The Ages of Gaia* (Oxford: Oxford University Press, 1979).
28 Friedrich Schleiermacher, *The Christian Faith*, 5.1,1 as quoted in Bruce L. Boyer, 'Schleiermacher and divine causality', *Religious Studies*, 22 (1986), 113–123.
29 Kevin W. Hector, 'Actualism and incarnation: the high Christology of Friedrich Schleiermacher', *International Journal of Systematic Theology*, 8 (2006), 307–322.

9 The recovery of nature's religious role in the context of the pandemic
Willemien Otten

The coronavirus pandemic has thrown scholars of religion and theology for a difficult loop. That is true both for more humanistic scholars of religion and theology and for more doctrinally oriented ones.[1] If ever a virus went not just global, turning from an epidemic into a pandemic, but also viral, manifesting itself through bouts of governmental concern and individual panic on the internet, the coronavirus did. As scholars of religion and theology, we have found ourselves dumbfounded in result. While we serve as a sounding board for human responses to the pandemic, we also feel called upon to address the intellectual quandary with which the pandemic confronts us professionally, showing us powerful (having caused it in some way) and vulnerable (being victimized by it) at once. The question now is whether we should accept this catastrophe as having thrown us off the precipice into a religion-less void or whether there is an appropriate religious line of questioning that can take us from a situation of nature in disarray to one where we can see nature as meaningfully imbued with the divine.

Beyond theodicy

In the past, humanistic religion scholars and more doctrinal theologians displayed different reactions to such crises. If theologians did not interpret any natural disaster as a divine warning or punishment for sinful conduct, they took it as the occasion for a theodicy, a justification of divine goodness. This was insightfully done by David Bentley Hart's *The Doors of the Sea. Where was God in the Tsunami?* after the 2004 tsunami in Thailand.[2] The parallel between the tsunami and God's frightening command of nature in the book of Job was not lost on Hart whose book is riddled with biblical references. Whether Leibniz's Enlightenment view of a "best possible world" that lies behind Voltaire's scathing parody after the earthquake of Lisbon in 1755, or Hart's Christian one after the 2004 tsunami, theodicies tend to analyze a disaster by theologically framing it. Yet in framing a catastrophe they ultimately subsume its upending of regular order under that same order, which then is called "natural." Natural as in "natural evil" thus carries the connotation not only of given, even if not manmade, but on a deeper level, of divinely permitted.[3]

It would seem that the Christian reaction to natural disasters as in the end more natural (that is, frameable according to the classical question of *unde malum*/whence evil?) than radically disruptive goes back at least as far as Augustine (354–430 CE). In *Confessions* 7 Augustine ponders the meaning of natural evil, considering it integral to what he calls "a conflict of interest in the universe."[4] What humans lack is the ability to oversee the cosmic integration into which, from a higher vantage point, any apparent conflict of interest is resolved.[5] The near impossibility of ever achieving such a bird's eye perspective, which for Augustine did not yet display the philosophical triumphalism that so irritated Voltaire after Lisbon, leads us to call such conflicts of interest evil. As in history, vis-à-vis which Augustine takes an anti-apocalyptic stance, as he compares the ages of history to the six days of creation in a "world week" that take us from the first day/age of Adam to the sixth day/age of Christ but never pinpoints the Sabbath, [6] so in nature he likewise shies away from calling out God's hidden plans. Our knowledge of the created order is provisional until it is revealed at the end of times. To aid the human mind, which fails to fathom how God according to Eccl. 18:1 created all things at once (*omnia simul*), the Bible categorizes nature's wonders according to the days of creation. Using scripture as the lens through which to read the natural order, Augustine pens many commentaries on Genesis, but no cosmological tract.

A more sacramental take on the pandemic is to find signs of hope and grace in the doctors and health workers who put their own lives on the line to help and assist patients.[7] In embodying a preternatural goodness, their sacrificial attitude is the inverse of how Augustine defines moral evil in *Confessions* 7.[8] After Adam's fall, humanity's divided will leads us to commit evil even though we know we should not. In the case of the health workers, they engage in the reverse, doing acts of preternatural goodness while it puts them at heightened risk. Insofar as their providing of care at their own peril benefits the community at large, there is a Christological aspect to their sacrifice. But no vicarious atonement can stop the rage of the pandemic, as long as no vaccine has been found.

The above sketch shows that traditional religio-theological responses to natural evil are inadequate to deal with the current pandemic. Insofar as we cannot frame or isolate this pandemic, as we are instead forced to socially distance and isolate ourselves, the virus and the socio-economic crisis it has unleashed force us to redefine the work of theodicy. Because the pandemic results from both natural mutations and human actions, it defies the separation of evil as either natural or moral. What seems to be needed is a fundamental update of the religious take on nature that bridges these classical bifurcations (natural-moral, nature-culture) through a deeper discernment of nature as religiously meaningful. Insofar as Christianity equates nature with biblical creation and defines the latter as the object of both God's creative act and humanity's stewardship, since according to Gen. 1:26 humanity is created in God's image, Christians have tended to see nature as passive and non-agential, which makes it an empty canvas vis-à-vis the particular questions that the pandemic puts before us. For, does the pandemic not show us that nature's otherness is not reducible to the controllability of objecthood and humanity cannot simply replace God's role of omnipotent creator?

Nature's otherness: agent and ally

To sketch out an alternative approach to what I call nature's otherness, I will focus on nature's unique position as mediating between humanity and the divine. While this mediation does not make nature itself divine, insofar as its analysis involves the divine and places nature in the center, it makes dealing with nature at heart an issue of religious and theological interpretation, just as it involves at heart also an anthropological reading.[9] Conversely, leaving God and humanity out of nature's analysis cannot but yield an irresponsibly impoverished sense of nature.

I will first focus on nature's agency. Both in the current pandemic and in the crisis of climate change, it is imperative that humanity become attuned to nature's agency to accommodate the fluctuations of its give and take rather than abolish responsibility or surrender to apocalyptic panic. For this section I draw on the late antique Christian thinkers Boethius and Maximus the Confessor, who give us different takes on nature's role as a cosmic force and religious conduit. In the next section it is we who must be respecting nature's otherness by seeing her as ally. I draw on modern thinkers Emerson and William James to flesh out a sense of the universe as animated, as signaling things to us that we would do well to heed for our continued well-being. The idea of nature as our ally forces us to cultivate a chastened sense of human selfhood, a new *askesis*, not in a Weberian innerworldly sense of mastery but rooted in a wider religious world-awareness that I consider an indispensable step in trying to overcome not only the chasm between human nature and nature but also that between nature and culture that has done our world so much harm. I consider the idea of nature as ally particularly promising for the development of a richer theology of nature.

Premodern nature in Boethius (477–526 CE) and Maximus the Confessor (580–662 CE)

Boethius

The Christian Roman senator and philosopher Boethius and the Byzantine liturgist Maximus the Confessor offer us two different models of an agential nature with direct impact on human lives. Boethius is best known for his *Consolation of Philosophy*, written after he fell into disgrace with the Ostrogothic Emperor Theoderic and, his political fortunes upended, was imprisoned while awaiting death. While the *Consolation* is customarily read as a philosophical dialogue in which Boethius is interrogated by an allegorized Lady Philosophy, the Middle Ages treated it as a Christian, revelatory text, although Boethius never invokes the Bible. In their allegorizations of nature, medieval poets model Lady Nature on Boethius' Lady Philosophy.[10] If we adopt this medieval reading, we see that Philosophy does not just teach Boethius the wisdom of ancient philosophical schools, but reconciles him to his impending death by showing him the providential pattern of the cosmos.

In a poignant exchange in Book II, Lady Philosophy engages in role-playing with Boethius. Posing as Lady Fortune, she provides Boethius with a teachable moment when, under questioning, he admits he entered this world without fame and riches. Just as he eagerly went up on Fortune's wheel, admitting that what he acquired was really on loan from her, so he must go down with her as well. Restored to her own identity, Philosophy summarizes, "Good fortune deceives, but bad fortune enlightens," as she has made Boethius realize who his friends are.

What follows is a poem that captures the dynamic reign of the universe, a providential bond that is cosmic as well as social:

> Even as the world with steadfast trust
> takes its regular turns
> and warring potentials

> keep their perpetual truce,
> And Phoebus draws forth
> the rosy day with his golden chariot—
> Such that Moon-Phoebe rules
> the nights that Evening brings,
> Such that the avid sea constrains
> its surges at a firm limit
> Lest lands wandering
> strive for broader bounds—
> The Love that rules over the lands and sea
> and commands the sky
> binds that cycle of events.
> If that Love released its control,
> whatever now loves mutually
> will make war immediately,
> And the machine that all now in companionable
> trust impel with beautiful motions,
> they would vie to break.
> That Love likewise holds together
> peoples yoked in holy alliance,
> And it fastens marriage's mystery
> with chaste forms of love.
> It also dictates its justice
> to faithful companions.
> O happy humankind,
> if the love with which heaven is ruled
> would rule your hearts![11]

In the middle line of the poem Boethius identifies Love as binding the cycle of natural events. The cosmic bond of love, reflective of Platonic *eros*, arranges the elements and fixes the tides, while it also unites the people in treaties and marriage. The poem ends with a plea for humanity to mirror the loving reign of nature in their hearts, later beloved by Dante, which bears out my point that Boethius' philosophical consolation amounts to a cosmic reconciliation. With nature distinguished from fortune as well as from fate, Boethius recognizes that its providential harmony manifests the ordered wisdom of a loving creator.

In Boethius' poem we have the bird's eye perspective that Augustine lacks, as for Augustine nature is accessible only serially, through the six days of biblical creation. Observing it entire, Boethius lets Philosophy depict nature here as an active, immanent force that exudes divine love. Encompassing the universe, love's cosmic reign stretches wide but also deep into social institutions. Nature's loving agency unfolds as a set of providential ramifications of God's single creative act.

Maximus

Born a few decades after the Justinian plague, Maximus the Confessor shows us an altogether different view of nature's agency, in which Platonic *eros* is replaced by the salvific impact of Christ's incarnation.[12] In bringing out the role of Christ, Maximus returns us also to the importance of scripture. Yet he does not foreground it at the expense of nature, but engages both simultaneously. In *Ambigua* 10.17, Maximus comments on the Transfiguration, a gospel episode which shows Jesus Christ radiant in glory on a mountain top with Moses and Elijah, while the disciples Peter and John look on.[13] In commenting on the effect on the disciples of this momentary anticipation of the eschaton, Maximus links nature and scripture both to Christ's radiant clothing:

> They (Peter and John) were also taught that the *garments*, which became *dazzling white*, convey a symbol: first of the words of Holy Scripture, which at that moment became bright, clear, and transparent to them…. and, second, of creation itself ….now appearing in the variety of the different forms that constitute it, all declaring the power of the Creator Word, in the same way that a garment makes known the dignity of the one who wears it.[14]

It follows from Maximus' intuitive image that nature and scripture must yield convergent truths, given "that the two laws—the natural law and the written—are of equal value and equal dignity, that both of them reciprocally teach the same things, and that neither is superior to the other."[15]

The alignment with scripture gives nature an emancipated role in Maximus, allowing it to assume agency in helping humanity chart its way back to God. Appreciative of creation for its own worth without fear of a wanton, nonspiritual materialism, Maximus depicts a close bond between nature and Christ. For, Christ's incarnation is aimed at the salvation not only of humanity's existence but also of nature's. Rather than seeing the return to God as restoring a flawed creation, the development of rational beings in Maximus unfolds as a threefold procession from creation to the eschaton, or from "being" to "well-being," and onto "eternal well-being."[16] Here we detect another parallelism: Christology in Maximus has cosmic consequences, while cosmic life has a Christological core to it.

Maximus is the first Christian author to insist that nature, like scripture, not just receive and channel but, more actively, itself convey redemptive wholeness. With the cosmos serving as conduit of redemption, one could argue that nature's animate operations are ultimately propped up by their Christological thrust, just as the parallelism of nature and scripture is premised on the event of Christ's Transfiguration. While this may not undermine nature's agency, it reveals it as conditioned by Christ's cooperation, which is continued after his death and resurrection through the sacramental life of the church.

Modern nature in R. W. Emerson (1803–1882) and William James (1842–1910)

When a millennium after Maximus modernity ushers in a more scientific era, nature's agency becomes increasingly divorced from the divine.[17] Among the many changes brought about by the scientific study of nature is its diminished religious legibility, which has led to what we may call the death of nature. Thus, Karl Barth, a Swiss neo-orthodox Protestant theologian battling the forces of Nazi Germany, emphatically opposed natural theology, embracing God's revelation in scripture as the exclusive route to salvation.[18] Driven by the ecological crisis, secular thinker Bruno Latour has recently criticized nature's inherent instability, suggesting to replace it with "Gaia, a finally secular figure for nature."[19]

Dissenting from both these positions as, respectively, too one-sidedly theological and too one-sidedly secular, and naming cosmos, world, creation, reality, and nature interchangeably, I consider it more important that the legibility of nature in modernity involves religion alongside science. Maintaining a focus on nature's role as liaison between God and humanity, and therefore holding on to its religious and its anthropological (rather than Christological) role, I want my interpretation to enhance rather than abrogate nature's legibility.

In oblique alignment with Lynn White's analysis of the historical roots of our ecological crisis, I agree that "modern Western science was cast in a matrix of Christian theology."[20] Insofar as that adds to Christianity's culpability for ecological exploitation, I understand why White is attracted to St. Francis' equality of all creatures, a path taken up further in Pope Francis' recent ecological encyclical letter *Laudato si': On Care for Our Common Home*.[21] As Pope Francis lauds St. Francis: "The poverty and austerity of Saint Francis were no mere veneer of asceticism, but something much more radical: a refusal to turn reality into an object simply to be used and controlled."[22]

White's turn to St. Francis also alerts us to the deeper problem of mainstream theology, from which St. Francis' biographer Bonaventure would step away, as casting theological and scientific analysis into a scholastic, second-order language from which all religious affect is drained.[23] Boethius and Maximus are altogether freer and more imaginative in expressing themes related to the theology of nature, such as providence, love, and the garments of Jesus Christ as symbols for nature and scripture. Seeing nature as both religious and anthropological I want to read nature holistically, and abolish any unnecessary dichotomies.

It is by becoming attuned to nature that we open ourselves up to seeing it as our ally. But mainstream theology does not offer many resources for a theology of nature, let alone one that it considers nature as our ally. In my quest for more imaginative modern thinkers, I will therefore turn to American thinkers R. W. Emerson and William James. Long neglected, they have recently become rediscovered for their viable impetus to creative religious thought.[24] Taking them up in reverse historical order, I first turn to James as my modern counterpart to Boethius and next to Emerson as my modern counterpart to Maximus.

William James

William James seems an atypical choice for a view of nature as ally, since he is known to define religion in terms of the religious subject in *The Varieties of Religious Experience*.

> Religion, therefore, as I now ask you arbitrarily to take it, shall mean for us *the feelings, acts, and experiences of individual men in their solitude, so far as they apprehend themselves to stand in relation to whatever they may consider the divine.*[25]

In some ways James gives us the solitude that Boethius might have felt, even if the language of experience and feeling is decidedly modern. But individualistic experience is not all there is to religion in James, who later on amends his earlier definition.

> Were one asked to characterize the life of religion in the broadest and most general terms possible, one might say that it consists of the belief that there is an unseen order, and that our supreme good lies in harmoniously adjusting ourselves thereto. This belief and this adjustment are the religious attitude in the soul.[26]

It is this latter statement that points us to nature as ally.

Building on the above two Jamesian ingredients of religion, namely individual solitude and the belief in an unseen order, a third step points out how James analyzes the cosmos not just as religious but also relational. In his earlier essay, "The Sentiment of Rationality," James argues that faith creates its own verification to the point that a cosmos with the thinker's reaction to it will always be different from without it, meaning that this reaction, let's call it one's faith, affects the whole in which it is embedded.[27] At the end of the essay James addresses the question whether we live in a moral or an unmoral universe. "But nature has put into our hands two keys, by which we may test the lock: if we try the moral key *and it fits*, it is a moral lock; if we try the unmoral key and *it* fits, it is an unmoral lock."[28] While this answer seems to force an arbitrary moral distinction upon us, not unlike the arbitrary way in which James asks us to take religion in the opening of *Varieties*, it masks a deeper call for discernment. It is in alignment with that discernment that he says that "the ultimate philosophy must not be too strait-laced in form," but over and above the realm of propositions (read, the scholastic approach) there must be left "another realm into which the stifled soul may escape from pedantic scruples and indulge its own faith at its own risk...."[29] While James accepts that not everyone is religious, it is clear that for those who are the universe is a storied one, with faith authenticating one story as a place of belonging.

R. W. Emerson

When advocating to read nature's role as religiously meaningful, even in the context of the pandemic, I realize that my plea, if received in Jamesian fashion, would only be valid for those who acknowledge religion as an effective personal choice. This choice does not present itself as such for the earlier Emerson, who left the ordained ministry but not religion, as he sounds a more capacious, universal message to us. The subjectivity of religion and the verification of faith, so carefully unpacked by James, are in Emerson encompassed by and folded into nature. Nature exudes a near-Maximian cosmic vibe in Emerson, even if it is impersonal more than Christological. Yet the impersonal in Emerson is also what can make him sound familiar and even intimate, meeting another condition for seeing nature as ally.

Being the more mysterious, but also more capacious mind, I consider Emerson the American thinker most attuned to the dynamics of seeing nature as ally. Hence, I deem his thought best suited to conveying to us what a "theology of nature" can entail. Aware of the urgency of his message, Emerson periodically resorts to poetry and prophecy, rather than propositional logic, to make his points. For, due to what he calls their overfaith, "the poet, the prophet, has a higher value for what he utters than any hearer, and therefore it gets spoken."[30] A more religious way of putting this is to refer to Emerson's unusual appreciation for the institution of preaching, "the speech of man to men," which he treasures and considers one of the advantages of historical Christianity.[31] Clearly, something needs to be preached about nature, and Emerson heeds the call.

Three significant aspects of Emerson's thought qualify him to me as the most powerful resource available for a contemporary theology of nature. First, Emerson sees nature rather than history as our prime matrix for contact with the divine. This is clear from how he opens his first book *Nature*:

> Our age is retrospective. It builds the sepulchers of the fathers. It writes biographies, histories, and criticism. The foregoing generations beheld God and nature face to face; we, through their eyes. Why should we not also enjoy an original relation to the universe? Why should not we have a poetry and philosophy of insight and not of tradition, and a religion by revelation to us and not the history of theirs?[32]

Lacking Augustine's and Maximus' patience to wait for the eschaton, Emerson demands an original relation to the universe right now. He does so not as a matter of personal choice but through a collective human embrace of nature as providing us with exclusive access to the divine. It seems fair to say that our acceptance that life is grounded in nature is what ultimately constitutes religion for Emerson.

Second, given the above it is no surprise that nature in Emerson displays a majestic surplus value, through which it utterly vanquishes the nature-culture divide. As Emerson states in his essay "Nature": "If we consider how much we are nature's, we need not be superstitious about towns, as if that terrific or benefic force did not find us there also, and fashion cities. Nature who made the mason, made the house."[33] What Latour calls the instability of nature is in Emerson the avowal of its unbounded capaciousness, by virtue of which nature can harbor both the religious and the anthropological aspect in its fold. It is relevant to point out that, notwithstanding the demise of the parallelism of nature and scripture in secular modernity, nature in Emerson retains a lingering scriptural echo. This comes out in such interjections as "All things with which we deal, preach to us. What is a farm but a mute gospel?"[34] While such comments are few and far between, and do not betray a commitment to historical Christianity, they make clear that the divine resonance of nature lies just beneath the surface. It is up to us to scratch that surface.

Third, Emerson is a deeply circular thinker, meaning that he avoids both nostalgic restoration and the linearity of progress. As he tells us in the essay "Circles,"

> The natural world may be conceived of as a system of concentric circles, and we now and then detect in nature slight dislocations, which apprize us that this surface on which we now stand is not fixed. These manifold tenacious qualities, this chemistry and vegetation, these metals and animals, which seem to stand there for their own sake, are means and methods only—are words of God, and as fugitive as other words.[35]

What is significant about the Emersonian circle is that it is neither gyrating nor cyclical; it is never fully closed. Leading to ever greater openness, unfolding into ever greater generalizations, circular life marks Emersonian temporality or onwardness, thereby putting hope on our horizon.

Conclusion

To recover nature's religious role in the context of the pandemic, my plea is not just to retrieve nature's religious agency but to treat and respect nature as our ally and listen to its otherness. Since nature mediates between humanity and the divine, it behooves us to take its role seriously. Rather than prejudge nature, either by lamenting the pandemic in apocalyptic terms or by striving for blind control over it, we should watch, observe, exercise caution, then strike with precision when opportune. The mark of a good preacher, says Emerson, is "to convert life into truth."[36] As our truth-driven theodicies have failed to answer life's problems, potentially leading to a destructive cynicism that denies a role for religion altogether in thinking about nature, it may be more worthwhile to move on the Emersonian circle, knowing that "Whilst the eternal generation of circles proceeds, the eternal generator abides."[37]

Notes

1 Note that I do not separate scholars of religion and those of theology per se but see more of a dividing line based on the degree to which scholars in either category are ideologically invested. My appeal is to those less ideologically inclined.

2 David Bentley Hart, *The Doors of the Sea. Where Was God in the Tsunami?* (Grand Rapids, MI: Eerdmans, 2019).
3 For relevant background reading on theodicy, which Leibniz had used as a title in 1710, see Terrence W. Tilley, *The Evils of Theodicy* (Eugene, OR: Wipf and Stock, 2000), 221–255 and Nicholas T. Wright, *History and Eschatology. Jesus and the Promise of Natural Theology. The 2018 Gifford Lectures* (Waco, TX: Baylor University Press, 2019), 3–41.
4 Augustine, *Confessions*, 7.13.19, transl. Henry Chadwick (Oxford: Oxford University Press, 1991), 125.
5 Idem:

> I no longer wished individual things to be better, because I considered the totality. Superior things are self-evidently better than inferior. Yet with a sounder judgement I held that all things taken together are better than superior things by themselves.

6 See *City of God* 22.30, transl. Henry Bettenson (London: Penguin, 1984), 1087–1091.
7 Augustine defines sacraments as "visible signs of invisible reality," see Emmanuel J. Cutrone, "Sacraments," in *Augustine through the Ages*, ed. Allan D. Fitzgerald (Grand Rapids, MI: Eerdmans, 1999), 744–745.
8 *Conf.* 7.16.22, transl. Henry Chadwick, 126: "I inquired what wickedness is; and I did not find a substance but a perversity of will away from the highest substance, you O God, towards inferior things...."
9 The anthropological aspect is what will lead us to bring up the nature-culture divide later in the essay.
10 This is especially the case in Alan of Lille's allegorical poem *Plaint of Nature* (ca. 1160), which had some influence on Chaucer. See further George D. Economou, *The Goddess Natura in Medieval Literature* (Notre Dame, IN: Notre Dame University Press, 2002), 28–52.
11 I am grateful to Michael I. Allen for this translation of Boethius, *The Consolation of Philosophy* II m. 8.
12 The Justinian plague raged in the 540s and was recurring through the mid-700s, killing between 25 and 100 million people and precipitating the fall of the Roman Empire.
13 See Matthew 17:1–8; Mark 9:2–8, Luke 9:28–36.
14 In his *Ambigua* ("Difficulties") Maximus explains contradictory passages from the Eastern theologians Gregory of Nazianzen (329–390 CE) and Dionysius the Areopagite (fl. 485–525 CE). For the parallelism of nature and scripture in *ambiguum* 10.17, see Maximos the Confessor, *On Difficulties in the Church Fathers. The Ambigua*, ed. Nicholas Constas (Cambridge, MA: Harvard University Press, 2014), vol. I: 193.
15 Idem., 195.
16 See *ambiguum* 7.10, ed. Nicholas Constas, vol. 1: 87.
17 But see the comment by Lynn White, Jr.: "From the 13th century onward, up to and including Leibniz and Newton, every scientist, in effect, explained his motivations in religious terms," in "The Historical Roots of Our Ecological Crisis," *Science*, New Series, Vol. 155, No. 3767 (March 10, 1967), 1206.
18 On Barth's famous debate about natural theology with Emil Brunner, see Alistair McGrath, *Emil Brunner. A Reappraisal* (Oxford: Blackwell, 2014), 90–132.

19 Bruno Latour, *Facing Gaia. Eight Lectures on the New Climatic Regime* (Cambridge: Polity Press, 2017), 7–40; 75–110.
20 White, "The Historical Roots of Our Ecological Crisis," 1206–1207.
21 See http://www.vatican.va/content/francesco/en/encyclicals/documents/papa-francesco_20150524_enciclica-laudato-si.html. Latour deems the move from St. Francis to *Laudato Si'* in accord with his own view of Gaia, see *Facing Gaia*, 287–288.
22 See *Laudato Si'*, end of section 11.
23 On the limitations of scholasticism in terms of topic rather than mode of discourse, marginalizing woman, the heretic, and the Jew, see Clare Monagle, *The Scholastic Project* (Kalamazoo, MI: Arc Humanities Press, 2017).
24 See Willemien Otten, *Thinking Nature and the Nature of Thinking. From Eriugena to Emerson* (Stanford, CA: Stanford University Press, 2020).
25 William James, *The Varieties of Religious Experience* (Cambridge, MA: Harvard University Press, 1985), 34 (James's italics).
26 James, *Varieties*, 51.
27 "The Sentiment of Rationality," in W. James, ed., *The Will to Believe and Other Essays in Popular Philosophy* (Cambridge, MA: Harvard University Press, 1979), 80–81.
28 Idem., 88.
29 Idem., 89.
30 Ralph W. Emerson, "Nature," in *Collected Works*, vol. 3 (Cambridge, MA: The Belknap Press of Harvard University Press, 1983), 109.
31 See "Divinity School Address," in *Collected Works*, vol. 1 (Cambridge, MA: The Belknap Press of Harvard University, 1971), 92.
32 See *Nature*, in *CW* 1, 7.
33 See "Nature," in *CW* 3, 106.
34 See *Nature*, in *CW* 1, 26.
35 See "Circles," in *Collected Works*, vol. 2 (Cambridge, MA: The Belknap Press of Harvard University Press, 1979), 186.
36 "Divinity School Address," in *CW* 1, 186.
37 "Circles," in *CW* 2, 188.

10 Listening to the pandemic

Decentering humans through silence and sound

Lisa H. Sideris

In his commentaries on the Genesis creation stories, Martin Luther interprets myriad unpleasant elements of nature as punishment for humans' fall into sin. Noxious plants with thorns and thistles, parasites and stinging insects, the killing behavior of predators, even the emergence of plague and pestilence—all of these are "but so many messengers which continually preach to us of sin and the wrath of God on its account."[1] This reading of nature, and others like it, have remarkable endurance. Many theologians have more or less followed suit over the centuries, including some contemporary eco-theologians who perceive evolutionary processes that engender suffering, strife, and discord in nature as symptomatic of a fallen state in need of restoration to an original harmony.[2] Secular versions of this interpretation are widespread among environmentalists who see the pandemic as retribution for human transgressions, including habitat destruction and trafficking in wildlife. There is truth, of course, to this diagnosis. COVID-19 almost certainly arrived by way of zoonosis—viral "spillover" from nonhumans to humans—leaping from bats to pangolins to humans, in a process abetted by long-term ecological disruption and the globalizing tendencies of modern life. The virus is not a random, unforeseeable event that befell us, science writer David Quammen argues. We made it.[3] Preventing future outbreaks will require significant changes in personal and collective behaviors that drive zoonotic transmission. It will demand that we acknowledge both the positive and negative dimensions of humans' profound and inescapable entanglement with evolutionary processes and other living creatures.

Interpretations of nature as meting out punishment have the potential to instill humility and courage in the face of a virus capable of grinding human civilization to a halt. Pope Francis has suggested that COVID-19, much like catastrophic bushfires that ravaged Australia in 2019 and 2020, is nature's response to our continuing failure to address ecological crises.[4] In a slightly different vein, philosopher Stephen Asma argues that viruses are neither good nor bad, but frighteningly neutral toward humans. Nature has no intrinsic value or meaning, Asma assumes. Nevertheless, personifying nature is useful for our survival: "Imagining our lives as a dramatic struggle with occasional enemies (microscopic and macroscopic) can help us change hearts and minds, embolden convictions, inspire sacrifice, and thereby change the actual outcome of epidemics and other trials and tribulations."[5] This mythopoetic tragedy of hubris punished by a nature—specifically, a rogue strand of viral RNA—still bears the imprint of an anthropocentric diagnosis, suggesting that natural processes conspire to chasten us. Put differently, imagining the virus as a pointed communiqué of nature's displeasure (even if we "know" that in reality nature has no inherent value) is not quite imaginative enough.

There is also a whiff of human exceptionalism to popular "good news" stories of nature rebounding in the midst of pandemic-induced lockdowns. Widely circulated reports and images of animals reclaiming city streets, or fish and birds returning to clear-running waters, foster a self-congratulatory illusion that a fleeting period of human inactivity is all that is required to heal and restore nature.[6] These and other tales of the pandemic's silver lining effectively draw attention to ourselves and our supposed sacrifice. Humans emerge as protagonists of the story, able to repair nature simply by withdrawing from it for a brief interlude. "With a few weeks' supply of shelf-stable foods and unhinged Netflix docuseries," *New York Times* critic Amanda Hess mockingly observes, "we can save the planet."[7]

Is it possible to acknowledge human complicity in creating the pandemic without centering ourselves in the story, either as heroes or villains? Can we affirm meaning and value in nature at this critical moment in our relationship with the nonhuman world, without defaulting to narratives that revolve around us? What sort of engagement with nature—what kinds of attitudes and practices—might we cultivate in order to divest some of our attention from the human enterprise and reinvest it in nature as its own source of transcendent beauty, value, and meaning? The slowdown of the human world in the midst of the pandemic has foregrounded sights and sounds in nature normally obscured by human activity. For many of us, lockdown conditions presented new opportunities for *observance* in both spiritual and secular meanings of the word. In what follows, I explore practices of attending to natural sights and soundscapes, particularly the behavior and voices of birds, as a decentering exercise, a sensual-spiritual discipline akin to prayer. As we will see, the details of these practices, and examples of how to engage them, suggest some fruitful areas of convergence between science and spirituality.

Attunement to these sights and sounds can work against a tendency to spin narratives around ourselves in the midst of crisis. In the face of ongoing uncertainty about the future, we can embrace these moments of unasked-for stillness as a chance to develop habits of watching and (especially) listening. At the time of this writing, it remains to be seen how and when the pandemic will run its course, and whether it will bring additional lockdowns. Whatever the future holds, there is lasting value to be found in listening and watching, and in the ethics of attention these practices can foster.

Listening to soundscapes

Researchers in the field of soundscape ecology, an area of study concerned with acoustic relationships between organisms and their environments, have coined the term "anthropophony" to designate the variety of sounds emitted by environments populated by humans (*anthropos* meaning human; *phone* meaning sound or voice). These sounds commonly include language, music, traffic, and the general clamor of our species going about its daily routines. Anthropophony can be coherent or chaotic, pleasant or unpleasant (at least to human ears). A parallel term for anthropophony is "biophony," the collective sonic creations of diverse organisms living in a particular biome, such as birds, insects, and amphibians. A third category, referred to as "geophony," encompasses nonbiological sounds in nature—wind and rain, running water or waves, seismic events and other movements of the Earth.

Animals in densely populated environments often find creative ways to adjust their vocalizations to the patterns of human-produced noise, but there are limits to how much or how quickly they can accommodate our behaviors. Widespread destruction of natural habitats, and the increasing ubiquity of humans in landscapes of every sort raise the specter of sonic extinction: the diminishment or loss of natural soundscapes. The very same conditions underlie the increasingly common transmission of viruses from animals to humans. Ecologist Bernie Krause, who has been recording natural sounds for decades, estimates that half of the soundscapes he has recorded have now gone quiet.[8] For ecologists attuned to soundscapes through years of practiced listening, aural shifts can signal trouble, as with the loss of certain nonhuman voices through extinction, the early arrival of others due to warmer springs, or a chorus of new sounds generated by introduced and novel species. Most of us, however, lack this basic attunement. "With our cultural focus primarily on visual experience and manifestation," Krause writes, "we seem to have lost the delicate balance informed by incorporating all of the senses in our awareness of place."[9]

The pandemic's temporary stilling of human noise and activity has brought the sounds of nature to the surface—or simply disclosed what was always there beneath the incessant anthropophony. These sounds include not only the voices of birds and other creatures, but signals emanating from the planet itself. In recent weeks, the reduction of vibrations and rumblings from routine human activities and transportation systems allowed seismologists to listen to the Earth's movements and tremors with less background noise. These sounds of the Earth and its living beings have been a source of interest to scientists, and a comforting and pleasant distraction for many laypeople during lockdown. However, one must be very cautious about positing an upside to a pandemic that has unleashed enormous suffering and hardship, much of it falling disproportionately on poor and marginalized communities. Not everyone has access to outdoor recreation; nor can everyone work from home or even isolate themselves to reduce their exposure to the virus. "Staying at home is a privilege. Social distancing is a privilege."[10] The disproportionate impacts of COVID-19 on low-income and minority communities mirror (and are in fact related to) those of climate change, and both can be considered facets of environmental injustice.[11] Moreover, the harassment of a black birder by white woman in Central Park earlier this year is a reminder that conceptions of the natural world and who belongs in it are, and always have been, racially charged.[12] Cultivating attention to nature is no panacea for these broader injustices and systemic failures.

And yet it remains true that the nearly universal presence of birds in our midst makes these creatures unusually accessible and endearing to many people, whether it is pigeons scavenging on city sidewalks, the distant honking of migrating geese, or the turquoise gleam of a robin's eggs tucked into the eaves. Enthusiasm for birdwatching has surged during the pandemic. In spring and summer this year, birdwatching agencies around the world reported a flood of inquiries from people wondering whether birds and other voices in nature have become livelier and louder this season. Birds easily attract us with their characteristic darting movements and a beady-eyed alertness that borders on self-parody. In this way, birds are virtuosos of "selving," a word coined by the poet Gerard Manley Hopkins to describe creatures enacting their own essences.[13] Selving, as Calista McRae puts it, is "how a living being epitomizes itself in everything it does."[14] Attention to the selving of birds is an occasion for what Iris Murdoch called unselfing: escape from the confinement of our own obsessive self-regard.[15] Unselfing is a project we can undertake deliberately by turning to nature as a way of ridding our minds, even if only briefly, from selfish preoccupations. Practiced watching, listening, and contemplative prayer are key elements of an ethics of attention, "that quality of attentive beholding that allows the Other, whether human or nonhuman, to stand forth in its otherness and difference."[16]

Bird augury

Birds have traditionally been revered as harbingers, teachers, and sentinels. "In the voices of birds we hear augury, portent, prophesy," biologist and nature writer David Haskell observes.[17] Researchers in the field of ethno-ornithology report that human-bird encounters are widely perceived as person-to-person interactions and kinship relations. "The personification of birds is found among all peoples."[18] Birds are especially good for thinking with. Their behavior provides important environmental clues, for they are adept at anticipating changes in weather, and many birds alert others, including members of other species, to the approach of a predator. They are also ecological indicators, meaning that the health and well-being of birds often signals the overall soundness, or deterioration, of an ecosystem. Think of eggshells thinned by pesticides like DDT, as documented by Rachel Carson in *Silent Spring*[19] (1962), or the use of canaries to detect carbon monoxide in coalmines, a practice that continued into the 1980s. In some cultures, birds are understood to help people cope with uncertainty in their lives and changes in the social, natural, or supernatural realm.[20] Birds deliver messages through behavioral cues and their mere presence, but vocalizations, and particularly bird calls (distinct from songs), are the "augural sign" most commonly monitored across cultures.[21] Songs are typically issued by males and contain musical messages regarding territory or mating availability. Calls are more prosaic, often consisting of just a syllable or phrase communicating a simple announcement or query between pairs, or between parents and offspring: "Where are you?" or "Here I am."

Of course, if we attend to birds, or nature generally, with the sole expectation of receiving auspicious or ominous messages about ourselves and our concerns, then we are not truly engaged in a practice of unselfing. Sign-bearing birds that are primarily callers rather than songsters (notably, owls, crows, ravens, raptors of various kinds) are often associated with death, both ecologically and mythologically, and across many cultures. Their calls elicit fear and awe at the ego-shattering thought that humans might serve as prey or carrion, that we too are edible. To perceive ourselves as part of this larger web of eating and being eaten is "to acknowledge our own animality and ecological vulnerability."[22] We can think of vulnerability not as an expression of evil portent but as signaling our shared bodily condition and reciprocity with something beyond ourselves.

These states of vulnerability and attentive receptivity are highly regarded in numerous accounts of contemplative practices and in the phenomenology of prayer. In the Christian tradition, the spiritual value of being still and watchful—a practice called *prosoche*—has roots in the "late third and early fourth centuries, when Christian monastics first entered into the silence and solitude of the Egyptian desert to search for God."[23] Honing one's attention and wonder toward the created world meant seeing things clearly, without the fetters of egotistical fixations.[24] Douglas Christie argues that *prosoche* holds great ecological promise for helping us recover a sense of our proper place and participation in nature's wholeness. Disciplined, prayerful attention is a familiar endeavor not only to monks but to certain poets and naturalists as well. Christie argues that Charles Darwin was singularly proficient at the art of *prosoche*, especially where birds were concerned. As he matured as a naturalist, from the time of his voyage on the Beagle in the 1830s to his publication of *The Origin of Species* in 1859, Darwin grew ever more attuned to the sights and sounds of birds, drawing on an "increasingly refined capacity to disappear" in order to gain entrance into the hidden worlds of other creatures.[25] We might speculate, as indeed some scholars have, that Darwin's practiced ability to humble and even efface himself before nature's inhabitants led him to espouse a scientific theory that erodes human exceptionalism and places our species firmly within the natural, evolving world.

Extreme attention as prayer

Disappearance and dissolution of the self is a prominent theme in many spiritual discourses on attention and prayer. Simone Weil understands extreme attention as a form of prayer, a kind of negative effort of kenosis in which the "I" disappears and the soul "empties itself of all its own content."[26] The deliberate diminution of the self as described by Weil is just the first stage of prayer, for "alongside the dissolution of the self, there needs to be attention directed outward, toward the other-than-self," writes Mark Freeman.[27] "Only then will one receive the existential nourishment and inspiration required for true creation to come forth."[28] Prayer that dwells too much in consciousness of sin can easily become another form of self-absorption, not unlike Luther's oddly anthropocentric reading of nature as delivering a stern lecture on human sinfulness. Weil warns that obsession with sin "gives us the feeling that we are evil, and a kind of pride sometimes finds a place in it."[29] Something in the human soul struggles against the process of unselfing, and, thus, whenever we succeed in focusing our attention, whether in prayer or in secular activities of unmixed concentration, we crush some tiny bit of evil in ourselves.

This turning away from self-preoccupation is affirmed in accounts of prayer that align it with "the deepest decentering of the self."[30] Often conceived as a practice of inwardness, prayer is perhaps better understood as an expression of creaturely enmeshment with the world beyond. How prayer is conducted—its repositioning of the one who prays in relation to this wider world—is more important than the content. The *how* of prayer is "the how of outwardness."[31] The power of turning toward the Other originates with something external to the self. The essence of prayer, then, is *response*. It is preceded always "by the one to whom it is addressed" and yet its outward intentionality effects a change in the sender rather than the addressee.[32] Prayer changes the one who prays.

Jean-Louis Chrétien understands prayer to commence with a posture of receptivity that is perhaps less a disappearance of the self than a state of extreme vulnerability that puts the self "thoroughly at stake."[33] Chrétien is especially interested in the *wounding* quality of praying. Prayer wounds precisely because it does not speak to or about oneself. Prayer disarms the ego in its implicit acknowledgment that the human is not the source or aim of all that is good. To be sure, Chrétien typically gives primacy to the *spoken* nature of prayer, but he recognizes the critical role of silent attending as an attitude of respect and adoration that transforms silence into prayer, an act of presence before the Other. "Silence is still allocution."[34] Chrétien refers to the initial posture before the Other as "anthropophany," where "-phany" indicates an appearance, opening, or exposure of the self before the divine. The anthropophanic manifestation of the self in prayer corresponds to theophany, that is, the manifestation or showing forth of God. Anthropophany exposes the one who prays, and yet the exposure has the quality of self-retreat, as one attends and awaits the Other in a state of radical passivity.

Listening as the gift of belonging

I am suggesting, then, that the discipline entailed in the patient waiting of one who watches and listens attentively to the natural world partakes of the kenotic movement—the self-emptying gesture—of prayer. In a silent echo of the bird's call—"Here I am"—the human listener responds much like Samuel to God: "Here I am, for you called me."[35] This voluntary decentering of the self expresses a willingness to be at the disposal of another. The notion of disposability intended here, Merold Westphal notes with humor, is not that of the "disposable diaper or the disposable contact lenses," but rather a statement of belonging: *I belong to you.*[36]

Does all of this sound a bit farfetched as a model for pandemic-borne practices of attending to nature? Can anyone really believe that a dramatic opening of the self in the presence of some radical non-human Other is attainable, or even desirable, for the average person, especially the person who finds herself weighed down by hardship and worry? In my own experience, it is precisely in such difficult moments that nature often speaks most eloquently. Murdoch, in her account of unselfing, similarly relates that in a mood of anxious brooding, she catches sight of a kestrel hovering in the sky. The brooding vanishes and along with it a preoccupation with "selfish care."[37] These welcome occasions of self-forgetfulness can remind us that we belong to something beyond ourselves.

As we have seen, the art of attunement to nature is a lifelong project. The details of Darwin's development as a naturalist attest to this. In this way, disciplined attention to nature does indeed resemble prayer, which is both the gift and the task "of a lifetime."[38] And yet, for all its disciplined effort, there is also something quite elementary about attending more closely to familiar creatures immediately around us. David Haskell offers a few simple listening practices for learning the language of birds. He advises letting go of the impulse to construct classifications and inventories, focusing instead on the distinct cadences, patterns, and textures of songs and calls.[39] Familiar and ubiquitous as they are, birds can seem quite alien. Their language is foreign to our species in a real, biological sense, and parsing it can be difficult, especially for beginners. Humans, as distant evolutionary relatives of birds, are equipped with distinctive mammalian auditory apparatus. The gulf between our species and theirs can be bridged by "the gift of our attention."[40] Haskell urges us to undertake listening as a kind of spiritual exercise whereby we come to appreciate that "every species has a sonic signature, and individuals within species have their own unique voices. In this diversity of acoustic expression are embedded many meanings."[41] Bird songs and calls are not the "dead clanking" or "utilitarian grunts" of genetically programmed Cartesian machines.[42] Birds are complex, perceptive, improvisational.

They are meaning-makers. With practice—in both a literal and spiritual sense—we can enter into what Haskell calls the "language of belonging."[43] The pandemic has provided an opportunity to cultivate the gift and task of a lifetime of listening, and of thereby belonging to something beyond ourselves.

Attunement: from biophony to biophany

We have seen that the initial opening up of the self toward another is sometimes labeled anthropophany. The surface resemblance of anthropophany and anthropophony, two words that feature humans centrally, is intriguing and suggestive—anthropo*phany* being a stance of humble receptivity to the presence and voice of another, and anthro*phony* as the collective human noise that often drowns out reception of nature's sounds. We might think of attentive listening and watching in nature as a counterweight to, or refuge from, the continuous noise and activity of anthropophony. Put differently, much as anthropophany marks a preparative movement toward theophany—a manifestation or revelation of the divine—so attunement to biophony might serve as a conduit for receiving what might appropriately be termed bio*phany*: a showing forth of the vital agency, the sacred quality, of nature and nonhuman life.

The work of poet and cartographer Tim Robinson, who died earlier this year from the novel coronavirus, suggests something similar. Alongside his gifts as a writer, artist, and consummate map-maker, he was an avid listener and observer of rock, wind, and water. Robinson was remarkably adept at detecting the age-old entwinement of human and nonhuman language that surfaces audibly in placenames and placelore (much of his work was an intimate study of western Ireland). He described his work not as geography but geophany, offering the following reflection: "A theophany is the showing forth, the manifestation, of God, or of a god; geophany therefore must be the showing forth of the earth."[44] Biophany, I suggest, like geophany, carries a sense of making plain what is often hidden in the landscape, not just visually, but aurally as well. Robinson considered walking to be the ideal mode of communicating with the landscape, "a spatial practice that renders his project of geophany at once Earth-bound and (literally) pedestrian."[45] Walking has long been invested with spiritual significance, as seen in rites of pilgrimage and in meditative walking practices that fine-tune awareness and non-ego focus. And as it happens, attentive outdoor walking, listening, and observing are some of the few activities still available to many of us in the wake of COVID-19.

Attunement, in its literal meaning, suggests putting oneself in tune, or adjusting to harmony of sound. Is attunement an appropriate response to the pandemic? To conceive of nature as harmonious, and of the task of humans as fitting ourselves into nature's preexisting accord, is perhaps too romantic, too reminiscent of the theologian's desire to treat any suggestion of discord in nature as an aberration introduced by human sin. But consider attunement in light of its etymological relationship to *atonement* (Latin, tonus: sound, tone). Attunement-as-atonement points to the need for reparations and reconciliation—a delicate process that often begins with allowing others to tell their own story. The pandemic is both a sign of human-inflicted harm to the natural world and an opportunity to overcome our estrangement by cultivating a sense of belonging. Listening to the sounds of nature—voices that call on us without necessarily speaking to or about us—might be just the decentering exercise we need to effect meaningful change in ourselves.

Notes

1 Martin Luther, *Commentary on Genesis: Luther on the Creation*, Vol. 1, trans. John Nicholas Lenker, Project Gutenberg, 2015, https://www.gutenberg.org/files/48193/48193-h/48193-h.htm#sect26.
2 Lisa H. Sideris, *Environmental Ethics, Ecological Theology, and Natural Selection* (New York: Columbia University Press, 2003).
3 David Quammen, "We Made the Coronavirus Epidemic," *New York Times*, January 28, 2020, https://www.nytimes.com/2020/01/28/opinion/coronavirus-china.html.
  The "we" here is problematic, for some humans are more responsible than others for these destructive practices.
4 Della Gallagher, "Pope Says Covid-19 Could Be Nature's 'Response' to Climate Change," *CNN World*, April 8, 2020, https://edition.cnn.com/world/live-news/coronavirus-pandemic-04-08-20/h_fa578270a745eb4e5b1321742a5a87f4.
5 Stephen Asma, "Does the Pandemic Have a Purpose?" *New York Times*, April 16, 2020, https://www.nytimes.com/2020/04/16/opinion/covid-philosophy.html.
6 These narratives problematically border on an ecofascist vision of a world without humans, or with human population sharply reduced—particularly, the eradication of already vulnerable humans.
7 Amanda Hess, "The Rise of the Coronavirus Nature Genre," *New York Times*, April 17, 2020, https://www.nytimes.com/2020/04/17/arts/coronavirus-nature-genre.html.
8 Bernie Krause, "A Lifetime of Listening," interview by Bruce Gellerman, *Living on Earth*, PRX, March 16, 2012, http://www.loe.org/shows/segments.html?programID=12-P13-00011&segmentID=7.
9 Bernie Krause, "Biophony," *Anthropocene Magazine*, August, 2017, https://anthropocenemagazine.org/2017/08/biophony/.

10 Charles M. Blow, "Social Distancing Is a Privilege," *New York Times*, April 5, 2020, https://www.nytimes.com/2020/04/05/opinion/coronavirus-social-distancing.html.
11 Katherine Bagley, "Connecting the Dots between Environmental Injustice and the Coronavirus," *Yale Environment 360*, May 7, 2020, https://e360.yale.edu/features/connecting-the-dots-between-environmental-injustice-and-the-coronavirus.
12 Andrea Thompson, "Black Birders Call out Racism, Say Nature Should Be for Everyone," *Scientific American*, June 5, 2020, https://www.scientificamerican.com/article/black-birders-call-out-racism-say-nature-should-be-for-everyone/.
13 Gerard Manley Hopkins, "As Kingfishers Catch Fire," in *Gerard Manley Hopkins: The Major Works* (New York: Oxford University Press, 1986), 129.
14 Calista McRae, "The Bird in the Window," *Boston Review*, January 3, 2020, http://bostonreview.net/arts-society/calista-mcrae-birds-window-strikes-cities.
15 Iris Murdoch, *The Sovereignty of Good* (London: Routledge, 1971), 82.
16 Mark Freeman, "Beholding and Being Beheld: Simone Weil, Iris Murdoch, and the Ethics of Attention," *The Humanistic Psychologist* 43 (2015): 160.
17 David Haskell, "The Voices of Birds and the Language of Belonging," *Emergence Magazine Podcast*, June 21, 2019, https://emergencemagazine.org/story/the-voices-of-birds-and-the-language-of-belonging/.
18 Felice S. Wyndham and Karen E. Park, "'Listen Carefully to the Voices of the Birds': A Comparative Review of Birds as Signs," *Journal of Ethnobiology* 38, no. 4 (2018): 534.
19 Rachel Carson, *Silent Spring* (Boston: Houghton Mifflin, 1962).
20 Wyndham and Park, "'Listen Carefully to the Voices of the Birds,'" 545–546.
21 Ibid., 543.
22 Val Plumwood, "Surviving a Crocodile Attack," *UTNE Reader*, July-August, 2000, https://www.utne.com/arts/being-prey.
23 Douglas E. Christie, *The Blue Sapphire of the Mind: Notes for a Contemplative Ecology* (New York: Oxford University Press, 2013), 142.
24 Christie, *Blue Sapphire*, 159.
25 Ibid., 169.
26 Simone Weil, *Waiting for God*, trans. Emma Craufurd (New York: Harper Perennial, 1992), 115.
27 Freeman, "Beholding and Being Beheld," 164.
28 Ibid., 164.
29 Weil, *Waiting for God*, 109.
30 Merold Westphal, "Prayer as the Posture of the Decentered Self," in *The Phenomenology of Prayer*, eds. Bruce Ellis Benson and Normal Wirzba (New York: Fordham University Press, 2005), 15.
31 Norman Wirzba, "Attention and Responsibility: The Work of Prayer," in *The Phenomenology of Prayer*, eds. Bruce Ellis Benson and Normal Wirzba (New York: Fordham University Press, 2005), 90.
32 Jean-Louis Chrétien, "The Wounded Word: The Phenomenology of Prayer," in *Phenomenology and the "Theological Turn": The French Debate*, ed. Dominique Janicaud (New York: Fordham University Press, 2000), 153, 158.

33 Chrétien, "Wounded Word," 150.
34 Ibid., 160.
35 Westphal, "Decentered Self," 17, referencing 1 Sam. 3:8.
36 Ibid., 23.
37 Murdoch, *The Sovereignty of Good*, 82.
38 Westphal, "Decentered Self," 30.
39 David Haskell, "Five Practices for Listening to the Language of Birds," *Emergence Magazine*, https://emergencemagazine.org/story/five-practices-for-listening-to-the-language-of-birds/.
40 David Haskell, "The Voices of Birds and the Language of Belonging," *Emergence Magazine Podcast*, June 21, 2019, https://emergencemagazine.org/story/the-voices-of-birds-and-the-language-of-belonging/.
41 Haskell, "Voices of Birds."
42 Ibid.
43 Ibid.
44 Tim Robinson, *Setting Foot on the Shores of Connemara and Other Writings* (Dublin: The Lilliput Press, 1996), 164.
45 Neal Alexander, "Theologies of the Wild: Contemporary Landscape Writing," *Journal of Modern Literature* 38, no. 4 (Summer 2015): 14.

Index

Note: Page numbers followed by "n" denote endnotes.

acoustic relationships 118
Agamben, Giorgio 80, 83, 84
agency: apocalypse and opportunity 25; heteronymic notion of 18; human and non-human 22; modern anthropocentric conceptualisation 20; modern buffered self 19–20; modern philosophical dismissal 96; non-human objects 19; self, pandemic and un-buffering 22–23
Alpine pastoral governance systems 95
Altspace program 32, 33, 39n7
anthropocene 30, 34, 37, 96
anthropocenic modernity 55
anthropophany
anthropophony 86, 118, 119, 122, 124
anti-Blackness 44
anti-racism 85
apocalypsis 24–26, 44, 54, 56, 105, 113; agency 25; authority 25–26; identity 24; and opportunity 24
apocalyptic 10, 25, 26, 54, 56, 104, 105, 113
apophatic mysticism 7; Dionysian apophaticism 8
Aquinas, Thomas 18, 86, 96
Aristotelian causation 19
Aristotle 64n17, 97
artificial intelligence 55
Asclepius 33, 36

Asma, Stephen 117
attunement 36, 37, 118, 119, 123–125, 124–125
"augural sign" 120
Augustine of Hippo 69; *Confessions* 7, 104
authority: apocalypse and opportunity 25–26; modern buffered self 20–21; self, pandemic and un-buffering 23
autonomous identity 19–21
Averroes 19, 27n13
awareness 12, 23, 43, 69, 119

Baboulias, Yiannis 77n55
Bacon, Francis 19, 20
Baldwin, James 44
bare life 83, 84
Barnabas 56–58
Barth, Karl 99, 109; *Church Dogmatics* 99
Bennett, Jane 13
Berry, Wendell 14
Bible 50, 88, 94, 104, 106
biodiversity collapse 37
biome 93, 99, 118
biophony 118, 124; geophony 118
birds 7, 34, 85, 117–123
Black Lives Matter 44, 84
Blake, William 8
Boethius 105–110, 106–108; *Consolation of Philosophy* 106
Böhme, Jacob 7–11, 14
Bonaventure 86, 110

Index

Bostrom, Nick 55
Brazil 93

Campagna, Federico 14
Camus, Albert 91; *La Peste* 91
capitalism 7, 14, 45, 46, 82; neoliberal capitalism 45
Caputo, John 61
carbon emissions 46
carbon trading 92
Carson, Rachel 120; *Silent Spring* 120
Cartesian dualisms 96
catastrophes 78–80
Centres for Disease Control in North America, Europe and Asia 91
Charpak, Nathalie 36
China 47
Chrétien, Jean-Louis 122
Christ 41, 55, 70, 99, 104, 108, 109
Christianity 2, 51, 56, 58, 97, 105
Christian theology 96, 98, 109
circumspection *(Umsicht)* 57
civilisation 1, 17, 54, 55; civilization
climate change 5, 17, 22, 46, 54, 63, 92, 96, 105, 119
climate regime 91–94
Cobb, John B. Jr. 50, 52n24
Collier, Paul 28n22
communitarian 85, 95
Coronavirus 2, 6, 29, 36, 42, 50, 54, 67, 78, 79, 103, 124; *see also* COVID-19 crisis
COVID-19 crisis 1; economic values 17; human ecology 94–95; isolation 30; large-scale social isolation 90; modern social imaginary 17; multidimensionality of 66; ontological turn to Gaia 95–99; public health crisis 90; quarantine 29; re-enchantment 17; SARS-CoV2 virus 90, 91; semi-conspiratorial view 80; social distancing 29; social relations 30–31; tele-haptic projects 32–33; touch 30; Trump's treatment of 46; vaccinate for 67; viral conclusion 99–100
creation, doctrine of 95–99; continuing creation 93, 98, 99, 116; doctrine of creation 95–99
creationism 98

Cusanus (Nicholas of Cusa) 86
cynicism 63, 113

darkness/dark ecology 5; apophatic mysticism 7; apophatic/negativa mysticism 8; evocations of 6; mythic imagery of 5; tenebrous temporality 7–9
Darwin, Charles 121; *The Origin of Species* 121
Deleuze, Gilles 44, 55
digital age 32, 55
digital communication 29–35
digital technology 33–35
Douglas, Mary 94

earth system science 97
Eckhart, Meister 8
ecological crisis 78, 92
"ecological ontology" 10
ecology/ecologism 86; apocalypse and opportunity 24–26; environmental humanities 2; framework of 2; modern buffered self 18–21; pandemic and un-buffering the self 21–23
economics 21, 44, 45, 46, 50, 51; economic balance 91; economic liberalism 84; economic meaning-value system 22
ecotherapy 38
Emerson, Ralph Waldo 109–113
emotion 20, 21, 23, 37, 66
enchantment 14, 17, 26
enmeshment 4, 13, 122
entanglement 23, 42, 48, 116
environmental, regulation 46, 94, 95; humanities; crisis; environmentalism; modern environmentalism 92
Epistle of Barnabas 56
equine-assisted therapy 35–36
Eriugena, John Scottus 86
eschatological attitude 60–63
eschatological justice 60–63
eschatology: Heidegger, Christian eschatology 56–60; time and justice 60–63
essence 60, 69, 72, 86, 88, 98, 99, 119, 122
event 4, 5, 12, 22, 43, 58, 60, 61, 78, 83, 84, 88, 90, 107, 118

evil (natural, moral) 58, 90, 104–105, 121, 122
existence 4, 9, 10, 11, 19, 29, 30, 70, 72, 73, 78, 81, 108
existentialism 61, 69; "existential ecology" 7

faith 54–56, 58, 74, 91, 111
farmers markets 92
Feuerbach, Ludwig 62
flourishing 2, 25, 36, 51, 63, 66, 67, 68, 70, 71, 74, 75
Floyd, George 45
Freeman, Mark 121

Gaia theory 88, 97, 99
gene editing 55
Gentzke, Joshua L. I. 4
Gnosticism 63
Graeber, David 96
greenhouse gas emissions 92

Hampton, Alexander J. B. 1, 3, 14
Harari, Yuval Noah 56
Harman, Graham 87
Hart, David Bentley 68, 103, 104; *The Doors of the Sea. Where was God in the Tsunami?* 103
Harvey, Peter 48
Haskell, David 120, 125
healing 33–38, 48, 70–73
Hebrew Bible 94
Heidegger, Martin 39n1, 54, 56–58, 61, 62; *Being and Time* 57; Dasein 57; Christian eschatology 56–60; "fallenness," human beings 72, 73; Heideggerean technocracy 82; *The Phenomenology of Religious Life* 58
Heisenberg, Walter 99
Hennessy, Peter 17
herd immunity 81
Hess, Amanda 117
Hindu, Trinitarian structure 97
Holy Communion 73–74
human and nonhuman 42
human ecology 90, 94–95
human flourishing 70
human health care 36, 70
human-nature relationship 21
human noise 118–119

human solidarity 79, 80
Hutton, James 97

identity: anthropocentric construction of 24; apocalypse and opportunity 24; modern buffered self 18–19; self, pandemic and un-buffering 21–22
incarnation 39, 99, 108
India, dharmic traditions of 68
Indonesia 93
inhumanity 42–45
intersectionalism 47
Islam 97
isolation 30; large-scale social isolation 90

James, William 105, 109–113; "The Sentiment of Rationality" 111; *The Varieties of Religious Experience* 110
John of Patmos 41
Judaism 97
justice 13, 45, 60–63

Kant, Immanuel 18, 27n8, 87
karmic cycle of being 97
Kearney, Richard 29; *Touch: Recovering our Most Vital Sense* 35
Keller, Catherine 6, 41
Kierkegaard, Søren 60, 62
King, Martin Luther 37, 116
Krause, Bernie 118, 119
Kristeva, Julia 31, 32; *Corriere della Serra* 31

labour 82, 87
Latour, Bruno 13, 79, 80, 87, 96, 109, 112
Leibniz, Gottfried Wilhelm 103
liberalism 82, 83, 84, 85
life 43, 99; dialectical processes of 71; human health 70; multidimensional unity of 69–72; theological vision of 66
listening, as gift of belonging 122–124
Louv, Richard 37; *Our Wild Calling: How Connecting with Animals Can Transform Our Lives—and Save Theirs* 37

Lovelock, James 97; Gaia theory 88, 97, 99

McGrath, Sean J. 54
McRae, Calista 119
Mammon 46
marine environment 92
Martinez-Alier, Juan 95
Marx, Karl 82
Maximus the Confessor 106–110
Merleau-Ponty, Maurice 12
Merton, Thomas 59, 64n15
metaphysical realism 96
metaphysics 5, 6, 17, 18, 49
Michaud, Derek A. 66
Milbank, John 78
Miller, Andrew M. 100n4
Milton, John 46, 47, 48; *Paradise Lost* 47
modern buffered self: agency 19–20; authority 20–21; identity 18–19
modern nature 109–113
modern social imaginary 17; broad framework of 22; self identity 22
moment 88; anti-racism 85; Athens, cross-religious conversation in 48–49; of axial shift 55; Christian community 58; darkness and abyss 5; eschatological time 61; genesis—chooses 49; of global grief and disruption 18; healer and healed 35; for pan-reflection 1; teleology 60; tenuous approach 14; thick darkness 5; of time 57; transformative possibility 1, 2
Morton, Timothy 4–6, 85, 87
motivations 67, 73
Muir, John 92
multidimensionality 66; multidimensional crisis 66; multidimensional health 75
multidimensional perspective 72–73
Müntzer, Thomas 62
Murdoch, Iris 120

naïve holism 4
natural disaster 90
natural evil 104, 105
nature: agency of 105, 108, 109; as ally 106, 110, 111; alternative approach 105; anthropocentric conceptualisation 2; anti-mechanistic vision 10; COVID-19 17; vs. culture 79; vs. culture duality 80; echoic vision of 8; false notion 86; and humanity 85–89; impressionistic approach 11; theology of 73, 74, 106, 110–112
Naturmystik 7, 9
New Being 70–73
Newtonianism 97
nihilism 63, 84
non-human objects 19
nonlife 42–44, 47
Northcott, Michael 90

'One Health' project 93
Orbán, Viktor 82
Ostfeld, Richard 42
Ostrom, Elinor 95
otherness/alterity 9, 38, 51, 105, 113, 120
Otten, Willemien 103

pandaemonium 42, 46; pandemonium
pandemic: agency 22–23; authority 23–24; cultural/natural of 84; digital pedagogy 33; GDP projections 22; identity 21–22; inhumanity 42–45; modern social imaginary 14; in multidimensional perspective 73–75; pandemonium city 45–51; physical proximity 32; political responses 80–81; shadow, symbology of 5–7; social imaginary 2, 4
panentheism 42, 43, 48–51
pan en theos 47–51
panic consumption 23
participation 17, 24, 25, 26, 49, 51, 69, 74, 83, 86, 87, 99, 121
Patrick, Dan 6
Paul 48, 56, 58, 59, 66
Plato 6
Platonic dichotomy 34
political responses 80–81
Pope Francis 5, 6, 95, 109, 116; *Laudato si': On Care for Our Common Home* 109

positivism 8
"post-traumatic stress symptoms" 66
Powers, Richard 38
prayer 38, 117, 120–123
premodern 14, 17–20, 24, 26, 96, 106–109
process theology 10, 18, 19, 43, 48–50
Pseudo-Dionysius the Aeropagite 8, 9, 20
public health 68, 74, 90
punishment 50, 103, 116

Quammen, David 116
quarantine 29, 66
quietism 59

Rappaport, Roy 94
Rawnsley, Hardwick 92
reciprocity principle 34, 38, 39
religion 2, 50, 74, 94, 95
revolution 55, 62, 92
Robinson, Tim 124
Roethke, Theodore 7, 12; "In a Dark Time" 7
Rohr, Richard 38
Roy, Arundhati 47, 48
Ruskin, John 82, 92

sacrament 104, 109, 114n7
St. Roch (Rocco) 36
salvation/redemption 55, 58, 68, 71–73, 108, 109
SARS-CoV2 virus 66, 90, 91, 94 (see also COVID entry)
scarcity 33, 86
Schelling, F.W.J. 61, 64n19
Schleiermacher, Friedrich 98, 99; *The Christian Faith* 98, 99
Scripture/Bible 56, 58, 71, 104, 108–110, 112
secularism 50
self: alteration 69; awareness 71; identity 69; pandemic disrupts 21; preoccupation 122; self identity 22; subject-object dynamic 18; ungrounding 10
selving 119, 120
Sideris, Lisa H. 116
silence unselfing 9, 34, 45, 121, 122

Slamani, Leïla 31
social distancing 29, 47
social imaginary 1, 2, 4, 6, 17, 21–26
social relations 30–31
somatic therapy 35
soundscape ecology 118–120
sovereignty 62, 87, 89
'Spanish flu' 90, 91
spiritualities 83–84
St. Francis of Assisi 74, 109, 110
symbiocene 34, 37

tactile communication 36
Taylor, Charles 17, 26n1
technology 2, 32–35, 37, 55
tele-haptic projects 32–33
tenebrosity 5, 7–10
Thacker, Eugene 4
theodicy 49, 50, 91, 103–105
theology
Thiessen, Annalea 1, 3
Thurman, Howard 38
Tillich, Paul 66, 69–75; Ground of Being 69, 70; *Systematic Theology* 72
time 60–63; eschatological attitude 60–63; uni-directedness of 60
touch: and digital communication 29–35; and ecological connection 35–39; equine-assisted therapy 35–36; in medical treatment 35; somatic therapy 35; tactile communication 36
transcendence 62, 69, 87, 88
transfiguration 108, 109
Trinity, doctrine of the 86–88
Tsing, Anna

unemployment 46, 81
Universal Basic Income 54
utopianism 60, 62

Van der Kolk, Bessel 36
Vidal, John 42
Villarreal, Luis P. 42
viral conclusion 99–100
viral transmission 74
virus 5, 42, 43, 45, 90, 91, 99–100, 103, 116

Voltaire 104
VR technology 34, 39n7

Weber, Max
Weberian bureaucratic control 82, 106
Weil, Simone 121, 122
Westphal, Merold 123
Whitehead, Alfred North 43, 99; *Process and Reality* 99
White, Lynn 2, 3n1, 13, 73, 74, 77n54, 109, 110

Williams, Rowan 69
Wordsworth, William 92
worker rights 79–81, 104
World Health Organisation 91, 93
Wuhan virology laboratory 90–91

xenophobia 23

Yusoff, Kathryn 44, 52n8

Zizek, Slavoj 5, 6, 82
zoonosis—viral development 91, 116